POSITIONING YOURSELF
to receive
HEALING

DOUG JONES

Positioning Yourself

To Receive Healing

By Doug Jones

Unless otherwise indicated, all Scripture quotations in this volume are from the *King James Version* of the Bible.

Second Printing 2003

ISBN 0-89276-965-3

In the U.S. write:
Kenneth Hagin Ministries
P.O. Box 50126
Tulsa, OK 74150-0126
1-888-28-FAITH
www.rhema.org

In Canada write:
Kenneth Hagin Ministries
P.O. Box 335, Station D,
Etobicoke (Toronto), Ontario
Canada, M9A 4X3

Contents

Why This Book Was Written

I was one of the featured speakers at a conference in Minnesota, and to my surprise, there seated in the middle of the audience was my friend with his wife. I had sensed something was not right. My friend had lost so much weight and at an alarming rate over the last few months.

As I returned to my hotel room on that cold, winter day, my heart was so grieved. Prior to the conference, I had questioned others, seeking to discover what the problem was, but no one knew. Speculations ran wild.

As I spoke, I felt compelled to seek them out and invite them out to lunch. Completing my lesson, I approached them and they were so kind to accept the invitation.

Tenderly, I began to inquire about his condition. Immediately he changed the subject, but out of my deep concern for his welfare, I probed again. This time I witnessed a pause, then a change of tone in his voice. As I sat there quietly for the next fifteen minutes, he and his wife shared with me the complete story.

Bleeding after bowel movements began slightly about twelve months previously. Giving it no thought and seeking no doctor's opinion, the man continued to experience problems, and the blood increased in volume. After approximately eleven months of suffering much pain and discomfort, his wife finally convinced him to seek medical attention.

After tests were run, the report was shocking: colon cancer. The doctor reported that the disease had gone undiagnosed too long and that the cancer was too wide-spread to be treated successfully. An operation was out of the question. This young man had waited too long.

Oh, how I wish that the Christian community would seek medical assistance early on when symptoms first appear!

Multitudes would be alive today, but so many get into denial and refuse to seek medical advice. Some see receiving medical attention as a lack of faith. How far from the truth they are.

With tears in this man's eyes, he asked for help. I will never forget his look of desperation. I knew I had only a short time. I encouraged him to contact me when I returned to Tulsa, and we would get together to begin the task at hand.

Oh, how I wish that the Christian community would seek medical assistance early on when symptoms first appear!

The "task" was one that I was all too familiar with. I knew that he was a born-again child of God. He had accepted Christ as his personal Savior long ago. But the issue at hand, the work to be done, was to move him into position to receive his healing.

Too often we are so quick to pray for Christians who are sick. Yes, if an emergency arises and a life is endangered, by all means we should pray and pray "now"! But when it comes to sickness, generally speaking, we must take the time to be certain that they are prepared and positioned properly to receive when hands are laid upon them.

Failure to prepare the sick properly often ends in unrealized results. Frustration sets in and dear Christians leave prayer line after prayer line confused and disappointed.

If we stop and think about this issue of moving people into proper position before we pray, each of us would acknowledge that we do know something about this subject. Think about it. When working with the lost, isn't it true that before we pray, we make sure that they are in proper position to receive the Lord into their lives? This is accomplished by proclaiming to them how much Jesus loves them and what He has done for them through His death, burial, and resurrection. Once the seeker accepts these fundamental truths, we know that it is time to pray. We know that he or she is in proper position to receive Jesus as Savior.

Failure to prepare the sick properly often ends in unrealized results. Frustration sets in and dear Christians leave prayer line after prayer line confused and disappointed.

Dear reader, it is knowledge that moves the lost into position to receive salvation, and it is knowledge that moves the sick into position to receive healing by faith.

There is another avenue besides faith by which healing can be obtained. I will refer to it as "the manifestations of the Holy Ghost" as described in First Corinthians 12:7 through 11. You will find that a discussion of this method is absent from this book.

However, for you who have need of healing or for you who wish to minister to other Christians who are in need of physical healing, this book is dedicated to you. In the pages ahead, you will find simple truths that one must embrace in order to be properly positioned to receive healing by faith.

It is my prayer for you that as you learn from the pages ahead, the eyes of your understanding will be opened to the truth, for we know that the truth sets us free.

1
chapter

The Primary Principle

In order to position ourselves to receive healing through faith, we must begin by discovering the answer to a very legitimate question: What knowledge must the sick accumulate in order to position themselves properly to receive healing?

I will never forget the day I received the first glimmer of light concerning this frequently asked question.

Consider the following phrase carefully: Teach the God-side first, then teach the man-side; it makes the man-side easier. Contained within this simple phrase are the truths that will assist us in obtaining our healing through faith. There is a God-side and a man-side to subjects. Since we desire increased results concerning healing, let's apply this phrase to healing.

In order to obtain healing, we must accumulate a degree of knowledge about our Heavenly Father if we are to comply with the requirements placed upon us as recipients.

Ignorance about the God-side or the man-side drastically limits our ability to obtain healing through faith.

Examples abound in the Word that reveal this primary principle of teaching the God-side first and then teaching the man-side. For example, Jesus said, *"A new commandment I give unto you, That ye love one another; as I have loved you, that ye also love one another"* (John 13:34). Notice the phrase, "as I have loved you." This implies that if we have not been taught how He loved us, then our ability to obey this command will be limited. It is clear that in order to love others, we are to simply imitate Jesus. But without knowing how He loved us, it becomes difficult for us to love others.

> *Teach the God-side first, then teach the man-side; it makes the man-side easier.*

It's sad to have to admit, but for years, I would encourage Christians to walk in love. Yet I saw very little of the love of God being manifested through their lives. I would get so frustrated and discouraged, wondering why they would not walk in love when they knew it was a commandment.

But when I saw this primary principle — Teach the God-side first, then teach the man-side; it makes the man-side easier — only then did I comprehend why compliance had been so limited. They were ignorant of the God-side — I had failed to teach them how He loved us!

When a Christian is encouraged to walk in love without first being introduced to how the Father loves him, he has no example to imitate. Therefore, he is limited to his personal conclusions as to how the love walk should be executed.

Concerning the marriage relationship, Paul said, *"Husbands, love your wives, even as Christ also loved the church, and gave himself for it"* (Eph. 5:25).

From this verse, husbands are instructed to love their wives *even as* Christ loved the Church. This now explains why so many husbands are having difficulty loving their wives as they should. They have never been taught how God loves them.

Knowledge must precede compliance. When husbands have been taught how God loves them and when they follow His example, loving their wives becomes easy. Therefore, the principle is clear: Teach the God-side first, then teach the man-side; it makes the man-side easier.

The Gospel as Proclaimed to the Lost

Another example that will bring understanding to this primary principle is the Gospel of salvation when proclaimed to the lost.

The God-side that must be proclaimed to the lost reveals how much God loves them, how much He cares for them, and that the depth of His love for them was expressed in the sacrifice of His only begotten Son (John 3:16).

We continue to proclaim to the lost that Jesus took their place and died on the Cross for them, and that through Him, they may obtain forgiveness of sin and eternal life. As we proclaim these truths, we are preaching, declaring, and proclaiming the God-side of salvation.

Once the God-side of the Gospel is embraced, it then becomes easy for the lost one to execute the instructions provided for him in Romans 10:9: *"That if thou shalt confess with thy mouth the Lord Jesus, and shalt believe in thine heart that God hath raised him from the dead, thou shalt be saved."*

The instructions found in this verse reveal the man-side of obtaining salvation. We must believe in our heart that God hath raised Jesus from the dead, and we must confess Him with our mouth.

If the lost one is still having difficulty obeying Romans 10:9, then we should provide him with more God-side material. The more God-side information a person has, the easier it becomes to do what God expects of him.

Oh, how the world needs to hear the Good News today! If they could only hear from saints who are unashamed to proclaim the depth of God's love for them and how valuable they are in God's sight. If they could only hear from saints who have experienced the love, joy, peace, and hope that comes from a true relationship with our Heavenly Father. It would make doing Romans 10:9 so much easier. If they only knew the God-side, what a difference it would make.

Teach the God-side first, then teach the man-side; it makes the man-side easier. This principle is a universal one. Whether we are talking about the subject of forgiveness, the subject of prayer, or the subject of marriage, there are things about our God that we must come to understand if we are to comply with the personal responsibilities that have been placed upon us.

A Time of Learning

Now that we understand this primary principle, it becomes clear that our ability to position ourselves properly for healing depends upon how teachable we are. Our willingness to learn and apply the principles revealed in the chapters ahead will determine the amount of results that will be obtained.

There is a very interesting verse found in the Gospel of Mark. Jesus said, *". . . Take heed what ye hear: with what measure ye mete, it shall be measured to you: and unto you that hear shall more be given."* (Mark 4:24)

The Amplified Bible renders this verse as "And he said to them, Be careful what you are hearing. The measure (of thought and study) you give (to the truth you hear) will be the measure (of virtue and knowledge) that comes back to you, and more (besides) will be given to you *who hear*."

From this verse, I have come to this conclusion: The degree of importance that we place upon what we hear determines the quantity and the quality of the fruit produced in our lives.

When little importance is placed upon the truths revealed, little fruit will be produced. On the other hand, the more importance that we place upon the truths revealed, the more results we will see.

> *The degree of importance that we place upon what we hear determines the quantity and the quality of the fruit produced in our lives.*

I encourage you to study carefully the truths that will be presented in this book. Give them consideration and, if found to be true, with all effort apply them until you are satisfied with the fruit produced.

2 chapter

Desire, Pray, Believe: A Spiritual Equation

Before we begin teaching about the God-side of healing, I would like to direct your attention to what I believe to be the man-side of the issue. In doing so, it will give you a hint as to the direction that we will be heading in the chapters ahead.

When it comes to obtaining healing by faith, there is a certain position that we must be in. This position is given to us by Jesus in Mark 11:24. Jesus stated firmly, *"Therefore I say unto you, What things soever ye desire, when ye pray, believe that ye receive them, and ye shall have them."*

Believing That We Receive When We Pray

Believing we receive when we pray is the position we must be in if we desire to be healed by faith. Jesus clearly stated that if we are in this position, "we shall have them." Understanding the importance of being in this position of believing we receive when we pray becomes clear as we put Mark 11:24 into a mathematical equation.

$$
\begin{array}{l}
\text{Desire} \\
+ \text{ Pray} \\
+ \text{ Believe that ye receive them} \\
\hline
= \text{ Ye shall have them}
\end{array}
$$

Through this equation, it is evident that Jesus did not promise results just because we *desire* to be healed. Likewise, He did not promise results just because we *pray* about our situation. However, "Ye shall have them" is promised to those who desire, pray, *and* believe that they receive when they pray. Therefore, in order to obtain healing through faith, we must be in the position of believing we receive when we pray.

Understanding this, it suddenly becomes clear why I had previously failed in my attempts to obtain results in the past. It was not because I had stopped believing I received. It was not because I had wavered. Rather, I had failed because I never entered into the realm of believing I received in the first place.

We cannot waver in an arena that we have never entered into in the first place. The realm that we are promised results in is the realm of believing that we receive when we pray.

If we only desire and pray about our situation, we find ourselves continually trying to *get* God to heal us. Dear reader, do we really understand the difference between trying to *get* God to heal us and believing that we receive when we pray?

The person who is trying to *get* God to heal him will think, talk, and act differently than the person who has prayed and believes that he received when he prayed.

The person who is trying to *get* God to heal him will participate in every healing line that is offered. But the person who has prayed and believes that he received will not go forward just because a prayer line is offered to him. He will sit in his seat and think to himself, "No need for me to go up there. I have already prayed, and I believe that I have received. I am not trying to *get* God to move on my behalf; He has already moved on my behalf. I believe that I received." This is the person who is positioned properly.

. . . do we really understand the difference between trying to GET God to heal us and believing that we receive when we pray?

Take Time To Locate People

I will let you in on a little secret of mine. As I speak with the sick, I am endeavoring to locate them. I want to determine what they believe and where they are in relationship to Mark 11:24. When I find that the only thing they have done is prayed, yet have not stepped into the realm of believing that they receive, I know immediately where my work must begin.

In order to minister to others effectively, we must first take the time to determine what they believe and where they are spiritually. Jesus examined people, and what He found determined what and how He ministered to them. Remember what Jesus said in John 16:12: *"I have yet many things to say unto you, but ye cannot bear them now."*

As the result of Jesus' examination of those He desired to teach, He chose to withhold things from them because He recognized that they were not able to comprehend all that He wanted to say to them at that time.

Jesus examined people, and what He found determined what and how He ministered to them.

Likewise, the Apostle Paul took time to examine people in order to locate them spiritually and then allowed what he discovered to bridle what he taught them.

For example, in Acts 17 we find Paul ministering to the people of Athens. As you read this account please note the emphasized portions.

ACTS 17:15-23

15 And they that conducted Paul brought him unto Athens: and receiving a commandment unto Silas and Timotheus for to come to him with all speed, they departed.

16 Now while Paul waited for them at Athens, his spirit was stirred in him, WHEN HE SAW the city wholly given to idolatry.

17 THEREFORE disputed he in the synagogue with the Jews, and with the devout persons, and in the market daily with them that met with him.

18 Then certain philosophers of the Epicureans, and of the Stoicks, encountered him. And some said, What will this babbler say? other some, He seemeth to be a setter forth of strange gods: because he

preached unto them Jesus, and the resurrection.

19 And they took him, and brought him unto
Areopagus, saying, May we know what this
new doctrine, whereof thou speakest, is?

20 For thou bringest certain strange things to
our ears: we would know therefore what
these things mean.

21 (For all the Athenians and strangers which
were there spent their time in nothing else,
but either to tell, or to hear some new
thing.)

22 Then Paul stood in the midst of Mars' hill,
and said, Ye men of Athens, I PERCEIVE
that in all things ye are too superstitious.

23 FOR AS I PASSED BY, AND BEHELD your
devotions, I found an altar with this
inscription, TO THE UNKNOWN GOD.
Whom therefore ye ignorantly worship,
him declare I unto you.

Notice it says in verses 16 and 17, "... *his spirit was
stirred in him, WHEN HE SAW the city wholly given to
idolatry. THEREFORE disputed he in the synagogue with
the Jews. . . .*"

Apparently, as Paul walked about, he saw that the city
was wholly given to idolatry. Therefore, what he spoke to
them about was directly affected by what he saw as he
walked among them.

Again, in verses 22 and 23, it is evident that Paul's message to the people was influenced by what he found them involved with.

When it comes to ministering to others, take time to examine them. Locate them and discover what they are believing. Doing so will enhance your effectiveness and reveal where your work should begin and what work you should actually be doing.

Failing to locate people before you begin to minister to them will result in much wasted time and effort. Locating people will pinpoint the area of their greatest need, thus enabling you to add to their beliefs what is necessary.

Likewise, take time to examine yourself. Ask yourself the questions: Where am I in relationship to Mark 11:24? Have I been guilty of desiring and praying only? Do I honestly believe that I received when I prayed? Self-examination locates us. It provides a starting point.

As you learn from the following chapters, locating yourself will become abundantly clear. Each thought will rest on the foundation of previous thoughts. If adjustments in your belief system become obvious, I encourage you to make the necessary changes.

chapter

Building Your Foundation

In order to understand the importance of teaching the God-side before teaching the man-side, I would like you to examine the following stair-step configuration. I am going to use this visual illustration throughout this book to bring understanding to the task at hand: getting people positioned to receive from God.

Observe that each step makes the next step possible. Each step makes the next step reachable. Because steps are missing, many find it tremendously difficult to reach the level of believing that they receive when they pray.

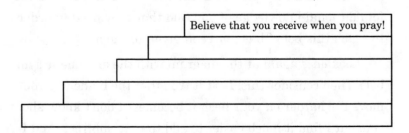

Believe that you receive when you pray!

For clarification concerning this concept of each level making the next level obtainable, consider the below diagram. Let's change each step into an arithmetic concept.

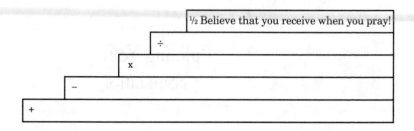

Understanding arithmetic as we do, we understand that knowing how to add aids us in reaching an understanding of how to subtract. Furthermore, knowing how to add and subtract assists us in reaching the level of multiplication. And it is clear that if it wasn't for adding, subtracting, and multiplication, it would be impossible to understand division. Consequently, adding, subtracting, multiplying, and dividing give us the necessary foundation for a clear understanding of performing simple algebraic equations, such as figuring fractions.

My point is this: The fraction level would be out of our reach had we not first learned how to add, subtract, multiply, and divide.

Such it is in most Christians' lives. Believing that they received when they prayed is out of their reach because the foundational knowledge of our God that they need in order to reach this belief has not been given to them.

Look once again at the diagram with the arithmetic symbols. Then consider this: Isn't it true that the higher up you move the harder on your flesh it becomes? I don't know about you, but I find it much easier to add than to subtract. And I would much rather add, subtract, multiply, and divide than do fractions. How about you?

Similarly, the higher we go in positioning ourselves to receive healing, the harder it will be on our flesh to accept. But as we take it step by step, we will find that the realm of believing we receive when we pray is within our capabilities. But without taking the proper steps, reaching the "fraction" level (of believing we receive when we pray) will seem impossible. And that is my very point: The realm of believing that we receive when we pray has seemed like an impossibility. But as we learn the foundational truths that support this belief, suddenly it becomes not only obtainable, but also easy to maintain.

The foundational truths found in the chapters ahead contain knowledge about our Heavenly Father. As we increase our knowledge about God, we are empowered to escape the grasp that ignorance has had on our lives. And we are able to reposition ourselves in the arena of believing we receive when we pray.

The realm of believing that we receive when we pray has seemed like an impossibility. But as we learn the foundational truths that support this belief, suddenly it becomes not only obtainable, but also easy to maintain.

4 chapter

The 'Must'
Factor

When it comes to healing there are certain things that
we *must* come to know about our Heavenly Father. As I
have ministered to the sick since 1975, I have become
increasingly aware of the fact that people have not failed to
receive healing because they do not believe. Rather, failure
has come in many cases because they do not believe what
they *must* believe.

Think about this. When it comes to being saved, there
are certain things we *must* believe about God. Romans 10:9
says, *"That if thou shalt confess with thy mouth the Lord
Jesus, and shalt believe in thine heart that God hath raised
him from the dead, thou shalt be saved."* In order to become
born again, we *must* believe "that God hath raised Jesus
from the dead." The lost cannot believe what they want to
believe and be saved; they *must* believe very specific things
about our God.

There are those who have chosen not to believe what
God requires. Rather than believing that God raised Jesus

from the dead and confessing Him with their mouth, they choose to believe that if they live a quiet life and don't lie, cheat, or steal that God won't send them to hell. However, the Bible does not teach that. The Bible teaches that in order for a person to be saved, he must believe what Romans 10:9 says and do what Romans 10:9 says to do.

'Should' Issues and 'Must' Issues

In life there are things we *should* do, and there are things we *must* do. For example, we *should* wash our car, but we *must* put gas in it. We *should* exercise, but we *must* eat. Likewise, there are things we *should* believe, and there are things we *must* believe in order to receive healing.

The scripture that exposed this idea of *must* beliefs to me was Hebrews 11:6, which says, *"But without faith it is impossible to please him: for he that cometh to God MUST believe that he is, and that he is a rewarder of them that diligently seek him."*

It appears that this verse is speaking of coming to our Heavenly Father to obtain something from Him. It gives strict instructions as to what we *must* believe when we come to Him in order to please Him.

> *. . . there are things we SHOULD believe, and there are things we MUST believe in order to receive healing.*

According to Hebrews 11:6, we are to believe that "He is" and that "He is a rewarder of them who diligently seek Him."

These two beliefs are not optional beliefs. He is not suggesting that we believe these things. Rather, we are told very bluntly that if we are going to please our Heavenly Father when we come to Him we *must* believe that He is and that He is a rewarder.

Notice that Hebrews 11:6 informs us that we are not to come to Him *to see if He is*. We are not to enter into a prayer line *to see if He is* a rewarder. No, my dear friend, it is plain — the beliefs that He is and that He is a rewarder are to be well formed within our lives long before we endeavor to step into His Presence. Entering into a prayer line during a church service just to see if anything is going to happen goes completely against what Hebrews 11:6 teaches.

Both Essential Beliefs Are To Be Equal in Size

Another issue that needs to be addressed concerning these two *must* beliefs from Hebrews 11:6 is that it appears that both beliefs are to be equal in size. In other words, we are not to have a strong belief that He is and a weak belief that He is a rewarder.

In order for these two beliefs to become equal in size, we must be taught as much about the fact that He is a rewarder as we have been taught that He is. Therefore, both subjects should be taught equally as strong and equally as clear.

We Must Know More About Our God Than We Know About Our Problem!

Let's read Hebrews 11:6 again: *"But without faith it is impossible to please him: for he that cometh to God must believe that he is, and that he is a rewarder of them that diligently seek him."*

When we come to God, we must believe that *He is* and that *He is a rewarder*. This implies that when we come to God we must know more about Him than we do our problem.

So many Christians today know more about their sickness than they know about their God. I have spoken with dear saints who have studied their illness to the degree that they have actually assisted the physicians in diagnosing their problem. They have studied their disease to the degree that they know what symptom is going to come next if the disease progresses. They know what medication to recommend for their treatment.

Knowing your enemy is a valid issue. I believe we should know all we can about the illness that is trying to destroy our lives. However, if we know more about our sickness than we know about our God, we have a real problem on our hands.

I see from Hebrews 11:6 that we are to know more about our God as we approach Him than we know about our problem.

We Must Believe That "He Is"!

The first God-side truth that we must understand if we are to reach the position of believing we receive when we pray is found in Hebrews 11:6. We must believe that "He is." I have looked at many different translations concerning this verse, and many of them translate this verse, "We must believe that He exists." The more I thought about this way of translating this verse, the more I disagreed with it. First of all, I wouldn't be coming to Him in the first place if I didn't believe that He existed!

The second reason why I do not believe that God is asking us to believe that He exists is, nowhere in the Bible does it ever set out to prove the existence of God. Think about it. If the Bible set out to prove the existence of God, would not Genesis chapter one have been written entirely different? Remember how this chapter begins: *"In the beginning God created the heaven and the earth. And the earth was without form, and void; and darkness was upon the face of the deep. And the Spirit of God moved upon the face of the waters. And God said, Let there be light: and there was light"* (vv. 1-3).

If the Bible set out to prove the existence of God, would not the beginning of Genesis have sounded something like this? "In the beginning God created the Heaven and the earth — oh, excuse me — I forgot you don't know that there is a God. Let me tell you about Him. Now you see, in the heavens lives this big guy by the name of God, and He has a lot of angels. . . ."

No, dear reader, the Bible does not begin in Genesis with a paragraph that tries to explain the existence of God. Rather, it goes directly into showing us how God created the world, and God said, and God said, and God said (vv. 3, 6, 9, 11, 14, 20, 24, 26).

Let's go back to Hebrews 11:6. What is God requiring of us when He says that when we come to Him, we must believe that "He is"? I will use the following example to help you understand. There was a time in my life when I believed that Jesus *was* the healer. I believed that Jesus healed in the Gospels but that He no longer healed today. Then someone came into the church I was attending and started teaching us that it is God's will for us to be well. As the result of this subject being clearly taught, I began to move from believing that He *was* a healer to believing that He *is* the healer.

I like to put it this way: After hearing that it is God's will for me to be healed, I switched from being a "*was*-er" to an "*is*-er."

The moment you believe that it is God's will for you to be well, you have met one of the conditions for pleasing Him. Once you believe that "He is" the healer, you have begun your journey toward believing that you receive when you pray.

The instant you believed that it is God's will for you to be saved, you met one of the conditions for pleasing Him. You believed that "He is"; you believed that "He is" the Savior.

Consider Figure 4.1. Knowing that our God is willing for us to be well is the first step that enables us to reach the belief that we receive when we pray.

Think about it from this standpoint: How would it be possible for us to ever step away from a healing line with the belief that we received if we were unsure as to whether or not it was God's will for us to be healed? It could not be done. So the first step that must be taken in order to reach the level of believing that we received is to learn that our God is willing for us to be healed.

Knowing that our God is willing for us to be well is the first step that enables us to reach the belief that we receive when we pray.

God's willingness is the first God-side truth that must be

embraced if we desire to reach the position of believing that
we receive when we pray. It is a foundational truth that
must be established in order for the belief that we received
when we prayed to exist in our lives.

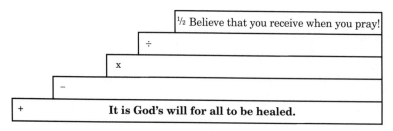

Figure 4.1

Therefore, the first thing I look for in a sick Christian is
whether or not he believes that it is God's will for him to be
well. Should I find this belief absent, I then know where to
begin my work and what I must teach.

5 chapter

It's God's
Will for You
To Be Well!

It is clear from our previous chapter that the first God-side principle that will aid us in reaching the position of believing that we receive when we pray is the fact that it is God's will for us to be well.

This belief must be formed within us from God's Word. Beliefs will always be the result of an accumulation of knowledge. The more scriptures that support this belief that it's God's will to heal, the stronger the belief becomes within us. However, so many have formed their beliefs based upon their own experiences or the experiences of others. It is sad, but experience can and has misled many into reaching improper conclusions.

Observe Figure 5.1. As I teach, I find it helpful to visualize the process of forming beliefs. As we form each belief, keep in mind that we are learning about our God so

Beliefs will always be the result of an accumulation of knowledge.

that we can reach with ease the belief that we receive when we pray.

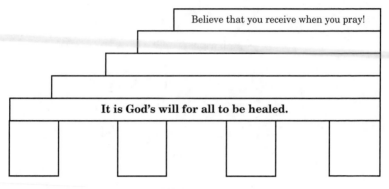

Figure 5.1

It Is God's Will That All Be Healed

There are four primary areas found throughout the Word that form the belief within us that it is God's will that we be well.

The first passages that support this belief are revealed in two Old Testament accounts: the Brazen Serpent and the Passover Lamb. Each of these aid us in believing that it is God's will for us to be well.

The Brazen Serpent

The Brazen Serpent is an Old Testament event that reveals what Jesus would do when He arrived on the earth. Jesus referred to this Himself in John 3:14 and 15.

John 3:14 and 15 says, *"And as Moses lifted up the serpent in the wilderness, even so must the Son of man be lifted up: That whosoever believeth in him should not perish, but have eternal life."*

It is clear that Jesus Himself implied that what the serpent did for the children of Israel, He Himself would do for the world through His crucifixion.

The account of the Brazen Serpent is found in Numbers 21:4-9.

NUMBERS 21:4-9

4 **And they journeyed from mount Hor by the way of the Red sea, to compass the land of Edom: and the soul of the people was much discouraged because of the way.**

5 **And the people spake against God, and against Moses, Wherefore have ye brought us up out of Egypt to die in the wilderness? for there is no bread, neither is there any water; and our soul loatheth this light bread.**

6 **And the Lord sent fiery serpents among the people, and they bit the people; and much people of Israel died.**

7 **Therefore the people came to Moses, and said, We have sinned, for we have spoken against the Lord, and against thee; pray unto the Lord, that he take away the serpents from us. And Moses prayed for the people.**

8 **And the Lord said unto Moses, Make thee a fiery serpent, and set it upon a pole: and it shall come to pass, that every one that is bitten, when he looketh upon it, shall live.**

9 And Moses made a serpent of brass, and put it upon a pole, and it came to pass, that if a serpent had bitten any man, when he beheld the serpent of brass, he lived.

Simply put, the people of Israel had sinned in their murmuring and complaining. Snakes were sent in among the people, and many were dying after being bitten by these snakes. Moses approached God to inquire as to what to do. Following God's instructions, he formed a serpent out of brass and placed it on a pole. God further informed Moses that whoever looked on the brazen serpent would be forgiven of their sin and healed from the snakebites.

Anyone who had been bitten could look upon this serpent and live. The brazen serpent was available for anyone who had sinned and for anyone who had been bitten.

Understanding this Old Testament account, let us reconsider what Jesus said in John 3:14 and 15. Jesus said, *"And as Moses lifted up the serpent in the wilderness, even so must the Son of man be lifted up: That whosoever believeth in him should not perish, but have eternal life."*

Jesus likened Himself to the brazen serpent. Therefore, we must conclude that any and all who have sinned, when they look to Jesus, can be forgiven. And any and all who need healing may also look to Jesus and expect to be healed. In other words, the benefits of the brazen serpent are the same benefits that are available to us through the crucifixion of Jesus.

Therefore, one reason for believing that it is God's will for all to be healed is revealed to us through this Old

Testament type. If what the brazen serpent did was for all of them, then what Jesus did was also for all. If through the brazen serpent, we can conclude that it was God's will for all to be well, then through Jesus we must also conclude that it is God's will for all to be well.

The Passover Lamb

There is a second illustration found in the Old Testament that also paints for us a picture of what Jesus has done for us through His crucifixion. Paul, writing to the Corinthians, refers to this event in First Corinthians 5:7, which says, *"Purge out therefore the old leaven, that ye may be a new lump, as ye are unleavened. For even Christ our passover is sacrificed for us."*

Paul calls Jesus "our Passover." Therefore, in the mind of Paul, what the Old Testament passover lamb did for the Israelites, Jesus would do for us through His crucifixion.

Let me refresh your memory as to the story of the Passover Lamb found in the Book of Exodus.

EXODUS 12:5-13

5 Your lamb shall be without blemish, a male of the first year: ye shall take it out from the sheep, or from the goats:

6 And ye shall keep it up until the fourteenth day of the same month: and the whole assembly of the congregation of Israel shall kill it in the evening.

7 And they shall take of the blood, and strike it on the two side posts and on the upper door post of the houses, wherein they shall eat it.

8 And they shall eat the flesh in that night, roast with fire, and unleavened bread; and with bitter herbs they shall eat it.

9 Eat not of it raw, nor sodden at all with water, but roast with fire; his head with his legs, and with the purtenance thereof.

10 And ye shall let nothing of it remain until the morning; and that which remaineth of it until the morning ye shall burn with fire.

11 And thus shall ye eat it; with your loins girded, your shoes on your feet, and your staff in your hand; and ye shall eat it in haste: it is the Lord's passover.

12 For I will pass through the land of Egypt this night, and will smite all the firstborn in the land of Egypt, both man and beast; and against all the gods of Egypt I will execute judgment: I am the Lord.

13 And the blood shall be to you for a token upon the houses where ye are: and when I see the blood, I will pass over you, and the plague shall not be upon you to destroy you, when I smite the land of Egypt.

It is clear that the passover lamb of the Old Testament did two things for the people. First, *anyone* who placed the blood of the lamb on his doorpost would be protected from the Lord's judgment. The blood protected any and all who were within the house.

The Lord did not see the blood on the doorposts and then peek into the house to see if there were any Egyptians within the house. No, this lamb's blood was available to any and all who would apply it. In reality, if an Egyptian would have followed the Lord's instructions, he, too, would have been protected from the judgment. Likewise, Jesus, our Passover Lamb, was slain, and all who accept Jesus as Lord will also be protected from judgment.

Secondly, the people were to eat of the passover lamb's body. This instruction prepared the people for their exodus. It brought physical strength and health to any and all who would follow the instructions.

Listen to what David the psalmist said about this subject of the Israelites' physical condition upon their exodus from Egypt.

PSALM 105:34-38

34 He [the Lord] **spake, and the locusts came, and caterpillers, and that without number,**

35 And did eat up all the herbs in their land, and devoured the fruit of their ground.

36 He smote also all the firstborn in their land, the chief of all their strength.

37 He brought them [the Israelites] **forth also with silver and gold: and there was not one feeble person among their tribes.**

38 Egypt was glad when they departed: for the fear of them fell upon them.

Notice verse 37, which says, *". . . and there was not one feeble person among their tribes."* How was this accomplished for a people that had just experienced almost four hundred years of captivity? It was accomplished through eating the body of the passover lamb. Anyone who ate was physically healed.

Jesus, our Passover Lamb, also shed His blood that we might be saved from judgment, and His body was broken for our physical well being.

David put it best in Psalm 103:1-4 when he proclaimed, *"Bless the Lord, O my soul: and all that is within me, bless his holy name. Bless the Lord, O my soul, and forget not all his benefits: Who forgiveth all thine iniquities; who healeth all thy diseases; Who redeemeth thy life from destruction; who crowneth thee with lovingkindness and tender mercies."*

> *The first place I begin forming the belief that it is God's will to heal all is with the stories of the Brazen Serpent and the Passover Lamb.*

What a blessed revelation! Through His death, Jesus provided freedom from judgment and sickness for all! The first place I begin forming the belief that it is God's will to heal all is with the stories of the Brazen Serpent and the Passover Lamb.

Let's add these two accounts to our visual illustration (Fig. 5.2).

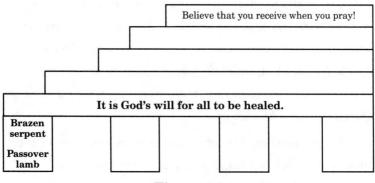

Figure 5.2

The Words of Jesus Reveal the Father's Will

Remember, there are four primary areas that support the fact that it is God's will to heal all. The first support is created from the accounts of the Brazen Serpent and the Passover Lamb. The second support that enables us to believe it is God's will to heal all is created from the words of Jesus. His words reveal the Father's will. What Jesus said was in essence the same words that the Father would have said if He had come to the earth personally.

Remember what Jesus declared in John 14:10: "*Believest thou not that I am in the Father, and the Father in me? the words that I speak unto you I speak not of myself: but the Father that dwelleth in me, he doeth the works.*"

Also in John 12:49, Jesus stated plainly, "*For I have not spoken of myself; but the Father which sent me, he gave me a commandment, what I should say, and what I should speak.*"

Let's read what Jesus says to the leper from the Gospel of Mark. Jesus reveals God's will for all who are in need of healing. Mark 1:40-43 says, *"And there came a leper to him, beseeching him, and kneeling down to him, and saying unto him, If thou wilt, thou canst make me clean. And Jesus, moved with compassion, put forth his hand, and touched him, and saith unto him, I will; be thou clean. And as soon as he had spoken, immediately the leprosy departed from him, and he was cleansed. And he straitly charged him, and forthwith sent him away."*

It is clear that this leper had become convinced that Jesus was *able* to heal. Yet one question had to be answered: Was He *willing*?

When questioned by the leper as to whether or not it was His will to heal, without hesitation, Jesus declared clearly, "I will; be thou clean." Notice that Jesus did not stop and pray to God to see whether or not it was God's will to heal. No, Jesus knew the Father so well that there was no need to inquire of Him in prayer concerning His will. Jesus knew that not only is it the Father's will to *save* all, but it is also the Fathers will to *heal* all.

Dear reader, do you understand the fact that what He will do for one, He will do for all? His clear, "I will" to the leper reveals plainly that it is God's will to heal all.

The Commissions of Jesus Reveal That It Is God's Will To Heal All

During the ministry of Jesus, He commissioned three groups to go and work on His behalf. Jesus sent out the Twelve — the first Apostles, His twelve disciples — the seventy, and then us, His Church. But before they went, He instructed them as to what they were to do and what they were not to do.

To all three groups, He gave a commission to heal the sick. Think about it. If it was not God's will to heal all, Jesus' instructions would have been with restrictions. However, there are no restrictions attached to these commissions. Jesus did not require the Twelve, seventy, or us to pray and seek God's direction before praying for the sick. Why? Because it is God's will for all to be healed.

Jesus did not require the Twelve, seventy, or us to pray and seek God's direction before praying for the sick. Why? Because it is God's will for all to be healed.

Take time to observe these three commissions. Notice the absence of concern that they might meet someone along the way who it was not God's will to heal. These commissions reveal clearly that it is God's will to heal all.

The Commission to the Twelve

Matthew 10:1 says, *"And when he had called unto him his twelve disciples, he gave them power against unclean spirits, to cast them out, AND TO HEAL ALL MANNER OF SICKNESS AND ALL MANNER OF DISEASE."*

The Commission to the Seventy

LUKE 10:1-9

1   **After these things the Lord appointed other seventy also, and sent them two and two before his face into every city and place, whither he himself would come.**

2 Therefore said he unto them, The harvest truly is great, but the labourers are few: pray ye therefore the Lord of the harvest, that he would send forth labourers into his harvest.

3 Go your ways: behold, I send you forth as lambs among wolves.

4 Carry neither purse, nor scrip, nor shoes: and salute no man by the way.

5 And into whatsoever house ye enter, first say, Peace be to this house.

6 And if the son of peace be there, your peace shall rest upon it: if not, it shall turn to you again.

7 And in the same house remain, eating and drinking such things as they give: for the labourer is worthy of his hire. Go not from house to house.

8 And into whatsoever city ye enter, and they receive you, eat such things as are set before you:

9 AND HEAL THE SICK THAT ARE THEREIN, and say unto them, The kingdom of God is come nigh unto you.

The Commission to Us, His Church

MARK 16:15-20

15 And he said unto them, Go ye into all the world, and preach the gospel to every creature.

16 He that believeth and is baptized shall be saved; but he that believeth not shall be damned.

17 And these signs shall follow them that believe; In my name shall they cast out devils; they shall speak with new tongues;

18 They shall take up serpents; and if they drink any deadly thing, it shall not hurt them; THEY SHALL LAY HANDS ON THE SICK, AND THEY SHALL RECOVER.

19 So then after the Lord had spoken unto them, he was received up into heaven, and sat on the right hand of God.

20 And they went forth, and preached every where, the Lord working with them, and confirming the word with signs following. Amen.

To the Twelve, Jesus commissioned that they "... *heal all manner of sickness and all manner of disease*" (Matt. 10:1). To the seventy, Jesus stated clearly, "... *heal the sick that are therein, and say unto them, The kingdom of God is come nigh unto you*" (Luke 10:9). And to the Church, He said, "... *they shall lay hands on the sick, and they shall recover*" (Mark 16:18).

The commissions speak for themselves: It is God's will to heal all! Glory!

These truths — the Brazen Serpent, the Passover Lamb, and the words of Jesus — enable the belief that it is God's will to heal all to exist within us. And without that belief, it would be next to impossible to believe that we received when we prayed. That's why we must teach the God-side first, then teach the man-side; it makes the man-side easier.

Now let's add to our illustration the fact that through the words of Jesus we can become persuaded that it is God's will to heal all (Fig. 5.3).

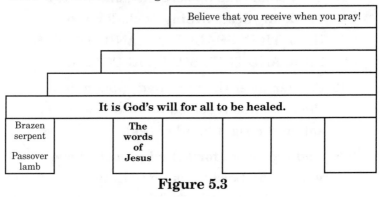

Figure 5.3

The third support truth that enables us to believe that it is God's will for all to be healed can be found through the *actions* of Jesus. Through the actions of Jesus, the will of God is revealed toward all.

Jesus Revealed the Will of God Through His Actions

. . . not one time was there a multitude large enough to have even one person whom it was not God's will to heal.

Jesus was the will of God in action. Jesus put it this way: ". . . *Have I been so long time with you, and yet hast thou not known me, Philip? he that hath seen me hath seen the Father; and how sayest thou then, Shew us the Father?*" (John 14:9)

Throughout the Gospels we find Jesus ministering to the multitudes. As we examine these occasions, we find that not one time was there a multitude large enough to have even one person whom it was not God's will to heal. Over and over, we see Jesus "heal them all."

For space sake, I will only show you the multitudes healed in the Book of Matthew. Doing so will ensure that we have no duplication of events.

MATTHEW 4:23,24

23 And Jesus went about all Galilee, teaching in their synagogues, and preaching the gospel of the kingdom, and healing all manner of sickness and all manner of disease among the people.

24 And his fame went throughout all Syria: and they brought unto him all sick people that were taken with divers diseases and torments, and those which were possessed with devils, and those which were lunatick, and those that had the palsy; AND HE HEALED THEM.

MATTHEW 8:16,17

16 When the even was come, they brought unto him many that were possessed with devils: and he cast out the spirits with his word, AND HEALED ALL THAT WERE SICK:

17 That it might be fulfilled which was spoken by Esaias the prophet, saying, Himself took our infirmities, and bare our sicknesses.

MATTHEW 9:35

35 And Jesus went about all the cities and villages, teaching in their synagogues, and preaching the gospel of the kingdom, AND HEALING EVERY SICKNESS AND EVERY DISEASE AMONG THE PEOPLE.

MATTHEW 14:14

14 And Jesus went forth, and saw a great multitude, and was moved with compassion toward them, AND HE HEALED THEIR SICK.

So we can now add another foundational truth to support the belief that it is God's will to heal all. The actions of Jesus reveal the willingness of the Father to heal all. Notice that the more support truths we know, the easier it is for us to believe that it is God's will for us to be well (Fig. 5.4).

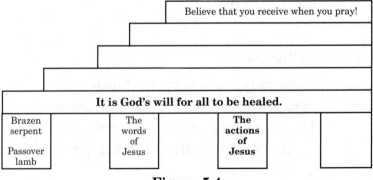

Figure 5.4

The fourth support that enables us to believe that it is God's will for all to be healed is what I refer to as the plan-of-redemption scriptures.

The Plan of Redemption Scriptures

Redemption was accomplished through the death, burial, and resurrection of our Lord Jesus. The following scriptures reveal what Jesus did for us through His death, burial, and resurrection. They reveal that not only did Jesus die for our spiritual salvation, but He also died so that we could be healed physically.

We know that Jesus died for all. Therefore, since the sacrifice was for all, then the benefits of His sacrifice are *also* for all. My friend, healing is for all!

Let's read some very familiar passages that enable us to believe that it is the will of God to heal all.

MATTHEW 8:16,17

16 **When the even was come, they brought unto him many that were possessed with devils: and he cast out the spirits with his word, and healed all that were sick:**

17 **That it might be fulfilled which was spoken by Esaias the prophet, saying, Himself took our infirmities, AND BARE OUR SICKNESSES.**

1 PETER 2:24

24 **Who his own self bare our sins in his own body on the tree, that we, being dead to**

sins, should live unto righteousness: **BY WHOSE STRIPES YE WERE HEALED.**

ISAIAH 53:3-5

3   He is despised and rejected of men; a man of sorrows, and acquainted with grief: and we hid as it were our faces from him; he was despised, and we esteemed him not.

4   Surely he hath borne our griefs, and carried our sorrows: yet we did esteem him stricken, smitten of God, and afflicted.

5   But he was wounded for our transgressions, he was bruised for our iniquities: the chastisement of our peace was upon him; **AND WITH HIS STRIPES WE ARE HEALED.**

PSALM 103:1-4

1   Bless the Lord, O my soul: and all that is within me, bless his holy name.

2   Bless the Lord, O my soul, **AND FORGET NOT ALL HIS BENEFITS:**

3   **WHO FORGIVETH ALL THINE INIQUITIES; WHO HEALETH ALL THY DISEASES;**

4   Who redeemeth thy life from destruction; who crowneth thee with lovingkindness and tender mercies.

It becomes clear through the previous verses that Jesus not only provided *salvation* through His sacrifice, but He also provided *healing* for the physical body. God's provision through Jesus for the healing of our bodies reveals His willingness to heal all.

Let's add this truth to our current illustration (Fig. 5.5).

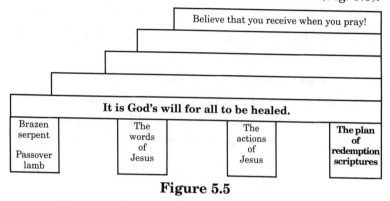

Believe that you receive when you pray!

It is God's will for all to be healed.

| Brazen serpent Passover lamb | | The words of Jesus | | The actions of Jesus | | The plan of redemption scriptures |

Figure 5.5

As you can clearly see, each support truth enables the belief that it is God's will for all to be healed to exist in our life. Once these truths have been embraced, we can move on to form the next belief necessary to reach our goal of believing we receive when we pray.

For those of us who desire to pass on to others what we believe concerning God's will to heal all, we must give them the truths that support our belief. So many of us encounter others who do not believe this basic truth about our God. Now we know what to give them in order to establish this fundamental belief within their lives.

Also, the truths that support our belief must be used to *defend* our belief — in this case, that it is God's will to heal all. Once we believe that it is God's will for us to be healed, doubts will come that will question whether or not it is God's will to heal all. When these doubts arise, we must defend our belief. This is accomplished by vocalizing what we know about the Brazen Serpent and the Passover Lamb accounts, by vocalizing what we know about the words and actions of Jesus which reveal the will of God, and by vocalizing our confidence in what the redemption scriptures have revealed to us. Doing so will cause the doubts to retreat, and we will find that it becomes easy to remain loyal to our belief that it is God's will to heal all.

If we are to reach the position of believing that we receive when we pray, we must become and remain confident of the fact that it is God's will to heal all, for it is a foundational truth that makes it possible for us to believe that we receive when we pray.

6
chapter

God — The
Liberal Giver

In the previous chapters, we learned that the first foundational step we must take to move toward the belief that we receive when we pray is *it is God's will to heal ALL.*

The second foundational step that moves us closer toward the belief that we receive when we pray is found in Hebrews 11:6: *"But without faith it is impossible to please him: for he that cometh to God must believe that he is, and that he is a rewarder of them that diligently seek him."*

Now that we believe that God *is,* we must move forward and include the belief that He is a rewarder. Believing that God is a rewarder is simply believing that God is a giver. One translation of Hebrews 11:6 says ". . . and believe that He cares enough to respond to those who come to him."

So if we are to please God, we must approach Him believing that it is His will that we be well *and* that He cares enough to respond to those who come to Him.

How could we believe that we receive if it was not God's will for us to be well? And how could we believe that we receive if we did not believe that God gives to us upon approach? It would be impossible! Think about it for a moment. The statement, "Believe you receive when you pray" implies plainly that you believe that something is given to you when you pray.

If God says that it is His will for us to be well, then we can be assured that *He is ready to give it when we ask.* And if He is not ready to give when we ask, He should not have promised it to us in the first place.

I found this principle to be true with my own children when they were little. If I told them that it was my will to take them for ice cream, I was prepared to give it to them right then. Because by the time I finished the sentence, they were in their bedrooms putting on their shoes and getting ready to go for ice cream! If you reveal that something is your will, then you must be prepared to deliver it when you are petitioned for it.

Before I accepted the Lord into my life, I heard preachers say many times that it was God's will for me to be saved. They convinced me that God wanted to save me. I was so convinced that when I walked up to the altar, I came with two beliefs. I believed that God is the Savior, and I believed that God would give me salvation when I asked. I came to him according to Hebrews 11:6 and didn't even know it! But I pleased Him with my coming, and He saved me. Glory!

If God says that it is His will for us to be well, then we can be assured that HE IS READY TO GIVE IT WHEN WE ASK.

However, when it comes to healing, it seems that most come with one belief only — that God wants them well. They lack the belief that God is a rewarder, that He is a giver. But consider this: Was not salvation and healing supplied to us through the same Sacrifice and at the same time? Does God not desire for us to be healed as much as He wants us saved? *Then why would we judge Him quick to give salvation to all who call, but slow to give healing to the sick?*

Scriptures To Form the Belief That God Is a Giver

We *must* believe that God is a giver. And we must not allow the experiences of others to form our opinion concerning whether or not God is a giver. We must go to the only true source of truth, and that is the Bible. We must allow *God's Word* to form our opinions about our God.

Now that we believe that it is God's will to heal, it becomes easy to believe that what He is willing for us to have, He will give upon request (Fig. 6.1). In order to reach the level of believing that we receive when we pray, not only must we believe that He is *willing*, but we must also believe that He is a *giver*.

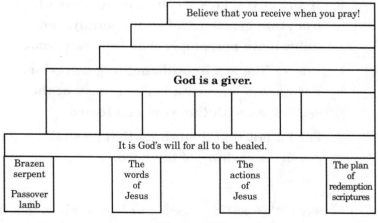

Figure 6.1

Once again, beliefs are the result of an accumulation of knowledge. Since God requires us to believe that He is a rewarder, we can be certain that there are plenty of scriptural passages we can accumulate to establish this belief within us.

James 1:5-7

The first scripture that comes to mind that teaches us that our Heavenly Father is a giver is found in James 1:5-7.

The connection between believing that God is a giver and our ability to believe that we receive is clearly established by James. The core thought of this passage is that if we do not believe that God is a giver, we cannot expect to receive what we have need of.

. . . beliefs are the result of an accumulation of knowledge.

JAMES 1:5-7

5 **If any of you lack wisdom, let him ask of God, that giveth to all men liberally, and upbraideth not; and it shall be given him.**

6 **But let him ask in faith, nothing wavering. For he that wavereth is like a wave of the sea driven with the wind and tossed.**

7 **For let not that man think that he shall receive any thing of the Lord.**

Let's read this portion of Scripture backwards so that it makes a little more sense. Now you can't do this with all scriptures, but there are a few that provide clarity when read "back to front."

Let's begin with verse 7, which says, *"For let not that man think that he shall receive any thing of the Lord."*

James has given the Church an awesome responsibility. He has instructed us to look into the lives of those who are petitioning God, and if we find them thinking in a particular way, we are to inform them that they should not think that they are going to receive anything from the Lord.

Since we have been given this responsibility, we must know what James is talking about. We must know what would disqualify someone from being able to believe they receive from God when they pray.

Verse 6 provides the answer: *"But let him ask in faith, nothing wavering. For he that wavereth is like a wave of the sea driven with the wind and tossed."*

James tells me that if I see you wavering, I am to inform you that you are not to continue to think that you are going to receive anything from God. People who waver will not receive their healing by faith. So if we desire to receive, we must guard against this enemy called wavering. Therefore, we must know what it means to waver.

In the past, I taught that the word "waver" meant *to go back and forth between two opinions*. But that is not what waver means in this verse.

The word "waver" means *to separate thoroughly*; *to oppose*; *to differ*; *to hesitate*. It means *to separate oneself in a hostile spirit*; *to strive with dispute*; *to contend with*.

When you are contending or differing with something, what are you doing? You are arguing with it, or as James puts it, you are *wavering*.

Therefore, James says that if I discover you arguing with something, if I find you contending with something, then I am to inform you that you are not going to receive anything of the Lord.

Now that we understand what this word "wavereth" means, we must ask the obvious question: What could you differ with that would cause me to inform you that you will not be receiving anything of the Lord? It is found in verse 5: *"If any of you lack wisdom, let him ask of God, that giveth to all men liberally, and upbraideth not: and it shall be given him."*

Take a pen and bracket off the following phrase in this verse: *". . . that giveth to all men liberally, and upbraideth not. . . ."*

Now what in verse 5 could you differ with that would cause me to have to inform you that you are not to think that you are going to receive anything of the Lord? I don't know about you, but I am not finding people differing with the fact that they lack wisdom. And I am not finding those who differ with the fact that God has the wisdom that they need. But I have found many who really do not believe that God will give to them what they have need of when they ask. So many people view God as a withholder and not a giver.

However, James informs us that if someone differs with the fact that God is a liberal giver, we are to inform the differing person that he is not to think that he will receive anything of the Lord.

After you have bracketed off the phrase in verse 5, could you not read it like this? "If any of you lack wisdom, let him ask of God, and it shall be given him." The phrase, *". . . that giveth to all men liberally and upbraideth not . . ."* is talking about God. It's giving us some information about our God that so many lack today. That information is that our God is a liberal giver.

James asked the question, "Are there any of you who lack wisdom?" He said, "If there are, ask God." But before James continued, he said, in effect, "Wait a minute. Let me give you some information about God before you go to Him and ask for wisdom. *God gives to all men liberally and upbraideth not."* Those who understand that God is a liberal giver will approach Him with a confidence that those who are ignorant of this fact could only dream of experiencing.

Let me illustrate the advantage we have when we know that our God is a liberal giver. Let's say that you needed to borrow some money from a bank, and one of your friends suggested you go see his banker. If he did not tell you anything about the banker he was sending you to, would you not approach the banker with a little uncertainty? Would you not approach him a little cautiously? But if your friend said to you, "Wait a minute. Before you go to my banker, let me tell you that he is a liberal giver. Every time I have ever sent anyone to him, he has always given him the money he needed without hesitation."

Now the question is this: Would that additional knowledge affect the way you approached that banker? Absolutely! Because of your knowledge that he is a liberal giver, you would approach him with a confidence that could not have been possible had your friend kept that information to himself. You would approach him with the assurance that your request would result in a positive, quick response. Glory!

Believing that our God is a liberal giver will affect the way we approach Him for healing.

Now if we think about it, we'll find that James is telling us the exact same thing that Hebrews 11:6 is saying — that when you approach God, you must believe that He is a giver. If you differ with that truth, you will not please Him, or as James puts it, you must be told that you are no longer to think that you are going to receive anything of the Lord.

Now, let's read James 1:5-8 in its entirety and see if this passage has become a little clearer.

> *Believing that our God is a liberal giver will affect the way we approach Him for healing.*

JAMES 1:5-8

5   If any of you lack wisdom, let him ask of God, that giveth to all men liberally, and upbraideth not; and it shall be given him.

6   But let him ask in faith, nothing wavering. For he that wavereth is like a wave of the sea driven with the wind and tossed.

7   For let not that man think that he shall receive any thing of the Lord.

8   A double minded man is unstable in all his ways.

Now that we understand verses 5 through 7, it becomes easy to comprehend what it means to be a double-minded man. He is the man that recognizes that he lacks wisdom. He looks to God and sees that God has the wisdom that he needs. So he approaches God and asks Him for wisdom. Yet as he is asking, he does not believe that God will give it to him. This man is double-minded and should not think that he will receive anything of the Lord, because he does not believe that God is a liberal giver. He does not believe that he will be given to upon approach. He is differing with the fact that God is a rewarder.

Let's apply this to the subject of healing. I know Christians who see their need for healing. They recognize that God has the healing that they so desperately need. Suddenly, the minister calls for those who need healing to come forward to have hands laid upon them. As others are moving forward, they think to themselves, *What's the use. I've had hands laid on me by the last four guest ministers. Nothing happened then, so why should I expect anything to happen now? God didn't do anything then, so why go forward this time? Well, I guess I will give it just one more try.* Do you see that they believe that God is, but they are differing with the fact that He is a liberal giver?

I had a person say to me as she pointed to a growth on her wrist, "Do you see this? I was prayed for three months ago, and God has not done anything about this yet." Do you understand that this person is differing with the fact that God is a liberal giver? This person does not believe that God is a rewarder of them who diligently seek him.

James admonishes us that we must believe that God is a liberal giver. Paul informs us in Hebrews that when we come to God, we must believe that He is a giver. It's time we understand that when we come to God for healing, we must believe not only that God is willing for us to be healed, but also that He gives to us upon approach. *Our God is a giver, not a withholder!* Glory!

I am talking about what it means to be a double-minded man. I know individuals who are Christians but they have sinned. They know that they have missed it. They know that they need to be forgiven. They know that God has the forgiveness that they need. So they approach God and ask for forgiveness. But all the time they are asking, they do not believe that God will forgive them. Once again, they are differing with the fact that God is a liberal giver. They are the double-minded man James talks about.

If we are going to please God, we must believe that He is a giver, and a liberal one at that.

Being 'Driven and Tossed'

Once I understood what this wavering was all about, suddenly, verse 6 caught my attention, especially the phrase, *". . . For he that wavereth is like a wave of the sea driven with the wind and tossed."*

JAMES 1:5-8

5   **If any of you lack wisdom, let him ask of God, that giveth to all men liberally, and upbraideth not; and it shall be given him.**

6   **But let him ask in faith, nothing wavering. For he that wavereth is like a wave of the sea driven with the wind and tossed.**

**7   For let not that man think that he shall
receive any thing of the Lord.**

**8   A double minded man is unstable in all his
ways.**

As I began to think about this, I said to the Lord, "I
understand what this word wavereth means. It means to
differ or contend with something. I understand that it does
not mean to go back and forth between two opinions. Since
this is true, why did You use the example of the wave to
describe the wavering one?"

I continued to think about this wave illustration, and I
thought, *Well a wave does go back and forth. But if the word
wavereth means "to differ," which implies "to argue against,"
why did James use this wave illustration?* Then, suddenly, I
heard these words on the inside of me: "Son, you've got your
eyes on the wrong thing. Take your eyes off the wave and
put them on being driven and tossed." The instant He said
that to me, I saw it! The individual who asks for wisdom
and yet, as he asks, does not believe that God will give it
will not receive. Therefore, he will continue to be driven and
tossed by his problems.

Oh, the multitudes of sick people who are being driven
and tossed by sickness and disease! We now understand
that it is the result of knowing that God is willing for us to
be well, but failing to believe that God will give to us upon
approach.

Remember Hebrews 11:6 requires us to believe that God
is and that He is a rewarder. Therefore, it is evident that

James 1:5-7 is our first scripture passage that establishes the belief within us that our God is a giver (Fig. 6.2).

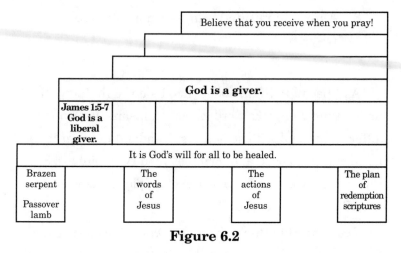

Figure 6.2

First Timothy 6:17

Remember, beliefs are formed as the result of an accumulation of knowledge. Another support truth we use to form the belief within us that God is giver is found in First Timothy. First Timothy 6:17 says, *"Charge them that are rich in this world, that they be not highminded, nor trust in uncertain riches, but in the living God, who giveth us richly all things to enjoy."* Paul is writing Timothy, who was pastoring the Church at Ephesus. He commissions Timothy to talk to those who are rich. Timothy is to encourage them to no longer trust in their riches, but to put their trust in God.

It seems very apparent to me that if the rich have been trusting in their riches and, suddenly, you suggest that they no longer do so, but rather trust in God, you had better give them some information about the One you're asking them to switch their trust to! So Paul instructs Timothy, "Since we are asking them to trust in God, let's tell them a little bit about God. Timothy, tell them that He gives to us richly all things to enjoy."

Timothy was to inform them that God is not a withholder. He is not selfish, tightfisted, or a penny-pincher but, rather, He is a giver. And He is not only a giver, but one who gives richly. So James calls our God a liberal giver (James 1:5), and now Paul calls him a rich giver (1 Tim. 6:17).

Let's apply this new support scripture to our visual illustration (Fig. 6.3).

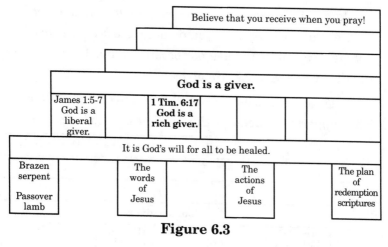

Figure 6.3

Romans 8:32

The third support truth that helps form within us this belief that our God is a giver is found in Romans.

Romans 8:32 says, *"He that spared not his own Son, but delivered him up for us all, how shall he not with him also freely give us all things?"*

How I wish we understood the depth of this scripture! The Father delivered the Son up for us all so that He could legally give us access to all that He has. Because He gave up his Son, we now have the privilege of partaking of and enjoying everything that the Father has provided for us.

My friend, since He loved us to the degree that He sacrificed His Son for us, how could we ever imagine Him saying no to us when we approach Him for healing.

No wonder Paul said in Second Corinthians 1:20: *"For all the promises of God in him are yea, and in him Amen, unto the glory of God by us."* Glory! All the promises are *yes!* Since they are yes, then He must be ready to give when we ask.

James 4:2 says, *". . . ye have not, because ye ask not."* Notice it did not say that you do not have *because He did not give.* He said you have not because you ask not, implying that when you ask, He gives.

Let's go back to our visual illustration (Fig. 6.4). Romans 8:32 supports the belief within us that our God is a giver.

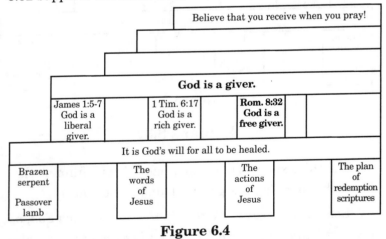

Figure 6.4

John 3:16

The subject of God the giver would not be complete without John 3:16.

John 3:16 says, *"For God so loved the world, that he gave his only begotten Son, that whosoever believeth in him should not perish, but have everlasting life."*

It was the giving nature of our Heavenly Father that attracted us as sinners to accept Jesus as our personal Lord and Savior. But for some reason we have allowed the giving nature of our Father to slip away from us. It is time to return to our first belief that our God is a giver — one who gives freely, richly, and liberally!

It was the giving nature of our Heavenly Father that attracted us as sinners to accept Jesus as our personal Lord and Savior.

After viewing Figure 6.5, it becomes easy to believe that God is a giver because we have scriptures from James, First Timothy, Romans, and John. The renewed mind can rejoice that the God we serve is not a withholder; He is a giver!

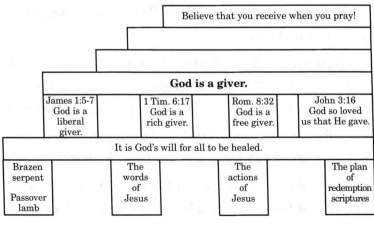

Believe that you receive when you pray!			
God is a giver.			
James 1:5-7 God is a liberal giver.	1 Tim. 6:17 God is a rich giver.	Rom. 8:32 God is a free giver.	John 3:16 God so loved us that He gave.
It is God's will for all to be healed.			
Brazen serpent Passover lamb	The words of Jesus	The actions of Jesus	The plan of redemption scriptures

Figure 6.5

God Is Our Father

When it comes to believing that our God is a giver, my thoughts turn to two terms that we use referring to our God. The first term is *Father*. I have been a father since 1982, and I have learned that it is impossible to be a father and not be a giver. Fathers are givers. They give of their wisdom and time. They give their love and money. And this is only the beginning of a very long list. True Christian fathers are givers.

Our God is called Father! He said in Second Corinthians 6:18 that He would be a Father unto us: *"And will be a Father unto you, and ye shall be my sons and daughters, saith the Lord Almighty."* Therefore, our God must be a giver.

God Is Love

Not only do we refer to our God as *Father*, but we also use the term *love* to describe our Father. God is love. Giving is the very nature of love. Where there is no giving, there can be no God-kind of love.

Remember John 3:16 which says, *"For God so loved the world, that he GAVE his only begotten Son, that whosoever believeth in him should not perish, but have everlasting life."*

Ephesians 5:25 says, *"Husbands, love your wives, even as Christ also loved the church, and GAVE himself for it."*

Love and giving go hand in hand. It's impossible to believe that God is a God of love and yet contend, or argue, with the fact that He is a giver.

No, Paul was not unjust in informing us that *". . . he that cometh to God must believe that he is, and that he is a rewarder of them that diligently seek him"* (Heb. 11:6). There is enough evidence in the Word to convince us that our God is a giver — and a liberal one at that.

Let's look at one more thought in Hebrews 11:6. Remember what this verse said? *"But without faith it is impossible to please him: for he that cometh to God must believe that he is, and that he is a rewarder of them that diligently seek him."*

Anytime you hear God commend a person for his faith after he received what he came for, you can be assured that he believed that "God is" and "He is a rewarder."

You understand that Jesus was God manifest in the flesh. Jesus said things such as, "If you have seen Me, you have seen My Father" (John 14:9). People who came to Jesus came to Him just as if they were coming to the Heavenly Father.

As we consider the healing records given to us in the Gospels, we should glean from them, learn from them, and then follow their example.

By the phrase "follow their example," I don't mean we are to do just what they did. If we had to do what they did, then before we could receive healing, we would be required to touch someone's hem or be lowered through a roof and so forth. Therefore, it becomes evident that the healing stories are not for the purpose of absolute duplication. So how do they profit us today? I like to say it this way: We are not to do exactly what they did, but we must believe what they believed. Let's look at several examples of sick ones who came to Jesus and see what they believed.

The Woman With the Issue Of Blood

The first example is the story of the woman with the issue of blood found in the Gospel of Mark. As you read this healing account, ask yourself two questions: Did she believe that Jesus is the healer? And did she believe that she would be given to upon approach?

MARK 5:25-34

25 And a certain woman, which had an issue of blood twelve years,

26 And had suffered many things of many physicians, and had spent all that she had, and was nothing bettered, but rather grew worse,

27 When she had heard of Jesus, came in the press behind, and touched his garment.

28 For she said, If I may touch but his clothes, I shall be whole.

29 And straightway the fountain of her blood was dried up; and she felt in her body that she was healed of that plague.

30 And Jesus, immediately knowing in himself that virtue had gone out of him, turned him about in the press, and said, Who touched my clothes?

31 And his disciples said unto him, Thou seest
the multitude thronging thee, and sayest
thou, Who touched me?

32 And he looked round about to see her that
had done this thing.

33 But the woman fearing and trembling, knowing what was done in her, came and fell
down before him, and told him all the truth.

34 And he said unto her, Daughter, thy faith
hath made thee whole; go in peace, and be
whole of thy plague.

As the woman pressed toward the garment of the Lord
Jesus, did she believe that He is the healer? Decidedly, yes!
Did she believe that she would be given to upon approach?
Absolutely — yes!

We know that she believed that He is the healer and that
she would be given to upon approach due to what she said in
verse 28: "*. . . If I may touch but his clothes, I shall be whole.*"

Her words were the result of what she believed. She
came to Jesus believing exactly what Hebrews 11:6 says
that we must believe. And as the result of her coming to
Jesus, Jesus turned toward her and said, "*. . . Daughter, thy
faith hath made thee whole; go in peace, and be whole of thy
plague*" (v. 34).

The Centurion Who Came on the Behalf of His Sick Servant

Another example of someone coming to Jesus for healing
is found in the Gospel of Luke. Here we find the centurion

who had a sick servant on the verge of death. As you read this healing account, ask yourself two questions: Did he believe that Jesus is the healer? And did he believe that he would be given to upon approach?

LUKE 7:1-10

1 Now when he had ended all his sayings in the audience of the people, he entered into Capernaum.

2 And a certain centurion's servant, who was dear unto him, was sick, and ready to die.

3 And when he heard of Jesus, he sent unto him the elders of the Jews, beseeching him that he would come and heal his servant.

4 And when they came to Jesus, they besought him instantly, saying, That he was worthy for whom he should do this:

5 For he loveth our nation, and he hath built us a synagogue.

6 Then Jesus went with them. And when he was now not far from the house, the centurion sent friends to him, saying unto him, Lord, trouble not thyself: for I am not worthy that thou shouldest enter under my roof:

7 Wherefore neither thought I myself worthy to come unto thee: but say in a word, and my servant shall be healed.

8 For I also am a man set under authority,
having under me soldiers, and I say unto
one, Go, and he goeth; and to another,
Come, and he cometh; and to my servant,
Do this, and he doeth it.

9 When Jesus heard these things, he marvelled at him, and turned him about, and
said unto the people that followed him, I
say unto you, I have not found so great
faith, no, not in Israel.

10 And they that were sent, returning to the
house, found the servant whole that had
been sick.

While this centurion anxiously waited on his dear sick
servant, someone testified to him about a man named
Jesus. The story was so convincing that the centurion
became persuaded that this Jesus is the healer.
Consequently, he sent a group of his friends with the mis-
sion of beseeching Jesus to come and heal his servant.

After they had been gone a while, someone noticed the
group of friends approaching from afar off. Eagerly, everyone rushed to the window to see if they had been successful
in convincing this Jesus to come.

Suddenly, the person who brought the testimony about
Jesus spotted Him in the crowd. And without hesitation, he
proclaimed the words that everyone in the room was long-
ing for: "There he is!"

The instant those words were spoken, the Centurion
knew that his dear servant would be healed without a

doubt. He quickly gathered a small group of close friends and sent them out to Jesus with a new message.

I can just see them now, running toward the group that's with Jesus. Half out of breath, the message is relayed to Jesus, "... *Lord, trouble not thyself: for I am not worthy that thou shouldest enter under my roof: Wherefore neither thought I myself worthy to come unto thee: but say in a word, and my servant shall be healed. For I also am a man set under authority, having under me soldiers, and I say unto one, Go, and he goeth; and to another, Come, and he cometh; and to my servant, Do this, and he doeth it"* (Luke 7:6-8).

As the crowd who was with Jesus listened to the message, it must have been received with amazement and wonder. But when Jesus heard the message, it must have been music to His ears. Never had he seen faith to such a degree, but, oh, how he must have longed to see more who exercised such faith!

Jesus was so delighted to hear evidence of such strong faith that Luke tells us that Jesus "marveled" at the centurion. He then turned to the people that followed him and said, "... *I have not found so great faith, no, not in Israel"* (v. 9).

The centurion must have followed the instructions, for we have no evidence that the centurion and Jesus ever met. Jesus spoke the word, and Luke tells us in verse 10 that "... *they that were sent, returning to the house, found the servant whole that had been sick."*

The point that I am making is that when we come to God, we must believe that He is and that He will give to us upon approach — that He is a giver.

Did this centurion believe that Jesus is the healer? I don't believe he would have sent the first group out to beseech Jesus if he questioned whether or not He is the healer.

Well, did the centurion believe that he would be given to upon approach?

... when we come to God, we must believe that He is and that He will give to us upon approach — that He is a giver.

Once again, how could he instruct Jesus to "speak the word only" if he did not believe that his servant would be given to freely.

The Man With Palsy Who Was Brought by Four

In Luke, I find another healing example that reveals clearly that the recipient came to Jesus according to Hebrews 11:6.

LUKE 5:17-26

17 And it came to pass on a certain day, as he was teaching, that there were Pharisees and doctors of the law sitting by, which were come out of every town of Galilee, and Judaea, and Jerusalem: and the power of the Lord was present to heal them.

18 And, behold, men brought in a bed a man which was taken with a palsy: and they sought means to bring him in, and to lay him before him.

19 And when they could not find by what way they might bring him in because of the

multitude, they went upon the housetop, and let him down through the tiling with his couch into the midst before Jesus.

20 And when he saw their faith, he said unto him, Man, thy sins are forgiven thee.

21 And the scribes and the Pharisees began to reason, saying, Who is this which speaketh blasphemies? Who can forgive sins, but God alone?

22 But when Jesus perceived their thoughts, he answering said unto them, What reason ye in your hearts?

23 Whether is easier, to say, Thy sins be forgiven thee; or to say, Rise up and walk?

24 But that ye may know that the Son of man hath power upon earth to forgive sins, (he said unto the sick of the palsy,) I say unto thee, Arise, and take up thy couch, and go into thine house.

25 And immediately he rose up before them, and took up that whereon he lay, and departed to his own house, glorifying God.

26 And they were all amazed, and they glorified God, and were filled with fear, saying, We have seen strange things to day.

Through their actions, we discover what this man and his friends believed. Their beliefs were so established and strong that they refused to be deterred. No crowd could stop them. No roof could cause them to abandon their beliefs.

As this group takes upon themselves the task of tearing a hole in the roof with the plan of lowering their friend into the midst before Jesus, it is obvious that what they believed was directly in accordance with Hebrews 11:6. They definitely believed that Jesus is the healer, and they unquestionably believed that they would be given to upon approach.

Jesus must have been pleased with their coming, for He never stopped them, nor did He try to discourage their efforts. Remember Hebrews 11:6 states that when you come to Him believing that He is and that He is a rewarder, it pleases God.

Through their actions, we understand that all the people involved in these three healing examples came to Jesus according to the path that was prescribed in Hebrews 11:6.

As we continue to think about Hebrews 11:6 and the instructions that it gives us, we must not become overly concerned about our ability to comply. For every child of God — every person who has accepted Jesus Christ as their Lord and Savior — came to God believing that He is and that He would give to them upon approach. If you're saved, you have already walked the path of believing that He is and that He is a giver. This is not some unfamiliar route that you have never traveled before.

We have come such a long way from only believing that it is God's will for us to be well. Because of God's Word, we have entered into an understanding that He is also a giver, and a liberal one at that.

Look at our visual illustration (Fig. 6.5) once again.

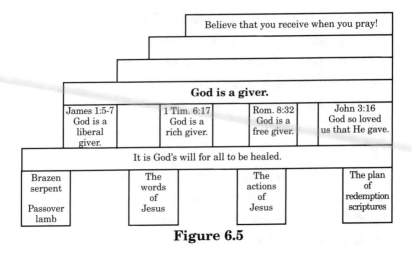

Figure 6.5

It is clear that each step makes the next step reachable. Learning that it is God's will for us to be well enables us to believe that He is a giver. Knowledge of His will must come first; then it is easy to believe that He will give to us upon approach.

To illustrate this principle, I'll use this example. Let's say that I am getting ready to re-roof my house, and I ask my best friend to help me. Without hesitation, he responds with a hearty, "Yes!" His positive response reveals that he is willing to assist me with the roof. But with that yes comes something more. The instant he said yes, what he really gave me was the knowledge that upon approach he would not deny me.

And that is my very point about our Father God. Since He reveals through His Word that it is His will that we be well physically, then what He is really saying is, "Upon approach, I will never say, 'No' or 'Wait awhile' to you."

No, my friend, since our Father says that He is willing for us to be well, you may be assured that you will be given to without hesitation. Our Father is a giver.

A Summary

Believing that our God is giver is established firmly by James 1:5-8, First Timothy 6:17, Romans 8:32, and John 3:16. Together they give this belief the solid right to exist in our life.

Secondly, the truths that support this belief are to be given to others who find it difficult to believe that our God is a liberal, free, and rich giver. It becomes easy to persuade others about what we believe when what we believe has been established within us from the Word of God.

Thirdly, the truths that support our belief must also be used to defend this belief. Once we believe that our Heavenly Father is a liberal, free, and rich giver, there will be doubts that arise that will question whether or not God is indeed a giver. When these doubts arise, we must defend our belief by vocalizing what we know about our giving Heavenly Father. Doing so will cause the doubts to retreat, and we will find that it becomes easy to remain loyal to our belief that God is a rewarder of those who diligently seek Him.

chapter

How God Gives to the Sick

Now that we understand that our God is willing that all be healed and that He will give upon approach, the obvious question that arises is, *How* does He give healing to us?

Consider the importance of this issue in light of the position that we must be in to obtain healing — the position of believing that we receive when we pray. We know that God is willing for us to be healed and that He will give upon approach, but through what vehicle does He give healing to the sick?

Throughout the Word, it is clear that there are a number of different methods through which God gives healing. I am going to mention a few that I find, and then, because of limited space, I will focus on what I consider the most prominent method.

Some of the methods through which God gives healing include:

**The Anointing of Oil and the Prayer of Faith —
James 5:14-16**

The Name of Jesus — Acts 3:1-10

Handkerchiefs and Aprons — Acts 19:11,12

The Spoken Word — Luke 7:1-10 and Mark 11:23

The Prayer of Faith — Mark 11:24

However, it seems to me that as I read the Word, the primary method through which God gives healing is through the laying on of hands. This truth is revealed throughout the ministry of Jesus.

Let's add this truth to our visual illustration (Fig. 7.1), and then, we will form this belief within you from scriptures.

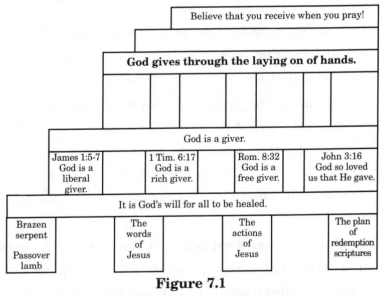

Figure 7.1

The Laying On of Hands

In observing the ministry of Jesus, it becomes evident that the primary method through which He gave healing to the sick was through the laying on of hands.

Mark 6:1-6

MARK 6:1-6

1 And he went out from thence, and came into his own country; and his disciples follow him.

2 And when the sabbath day was come, he began to teach in the synagogue: and many hearing him were astonished, saying, From whence hath this man these things? and what wisdom is this which is given unto him, that even such mighty works are wrought by his hands?

3 Is not this the carpenter, the son of Mary, the brother of James, and Joses, and of Juda, and Simon? and are not his sisters here with us? And they were offended at him.

4 But Jesus said unto them, A prophet is not without honour, but in his own country, and among his own kin, and in his own house.

5 And he could there do no mighty work, save that he laid his hands upon a few sick folk, and healed them.

6 And he marvelled because of their unbelief. And he went round about the villages, teaching.

Notice verse 5: "*And he could there do no mighty work, save that he laid his hands upon a few sick folk, and healed them.*"

Jesus believed in and used the laying on of hands to administer healing to the sick. It is one method through which God gives healing to the sick.

Let's add this support truth to our visual illustration (Fig. 7.2).

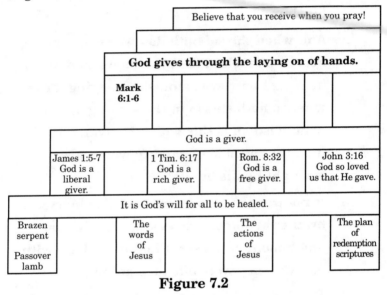

Figure 7.2

Mark 8:22-25

In Mark we find another piece of evidence that supports the belief that the laying on of hands is one way through which healing is given to the sick.

MARK 8:22-25

22 **And he cometh to Bethsaida; and they bring a blind man unto him, and besought him to touch him.**

23 **And he took the blind man by the hand, and led him out of the town; and when he**

had spit on his eyes, and put his hands upon him, he asked him if he saw ought.

24 And he looked up, and said, I see men as trees, walking.

25 After that he put his hands again upon his eyes, and made him look up: and he was restored, and saw every man clearly.

Jesus believed in and used the laying on of hands to administer healing to the sick.

Jesus laid his hands on the blind man. Jesus believed in this method. He believed that healing could be administered through the laying on of hands (Fig. 7.3).

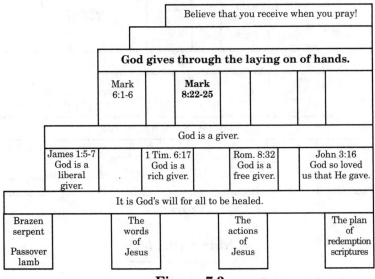

Believe that you receive when you pray!			
God gives through the laying on of hands.			
Mark 6:1-6	**Mark 8:22-25**		
God is a giver.			
James 1:5-7 God is a liberal giver.	1 Tim. 6:17 God is a rich giver.	Rom. 8:32 God is a free giver.	John 3:16 God so loved us that He gave.
It is God's will for all to be healed.			
Brazen serpent Passover lamb	The words of Jesus	The actions of Jesus	The plan of redemption scriptures

Figure 7.3

Luke 4:40

LUKE 4:40

40 Now when the sun was setting, all they that had any sick with divers diseases brought them unto him; and he laid his hands on every one of them, and healed them.

Here again is evidence that clearly reveals that the laying on of hands is a vital tool when ministering healing to others (Fig. 7.4).

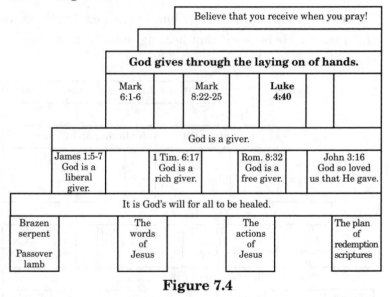

Believe that you receive when you pray!						
God gives through the laying on of hands.						
Mark 6:1-6		Mark 8:22-25		Luke 4:40		
God is a giver.						
James 1:5-7 God is a liberal giver.		1 Tim. 6:17 God is a rich giver.		Rom. 8:32 God is a free giver.		John 3:16 God so loved us that He gave.
It is God's will for all to be healed.						
Brazen serpent Passover lamb		The words of Jesus		The actions of Jesus		The plan of redemption scriptures

Figure 7.4

Mark 16:17-18

MARK 16:17-18

17 And these signs shall follow them that believe; In my name shall they cast out devils; they shall speak with new tongues;

18 They shall take up serpents; and if they drink any deadly thing, it shall not hurt them; they shall lay hands on the sick, and they shall recover.

Jesus believed in this method so much that He commissioned us, the Church, to use this method as we encounter the sick while spreading the Gospel (Fig. 7.5).

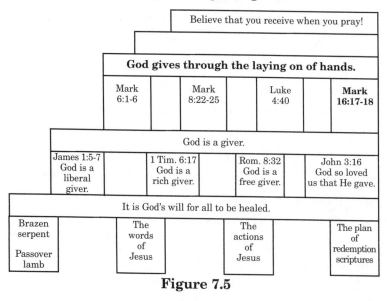

Believe that you receive when you pray!

God gives through the laying on of hands.

| Mark 6:1-6 | | Mark 8:22-25 | | Luke 4:40 | | **Mark 16:17-18** |

God is a giver.

| James 1:5-7 God is a liberal giver. | | 1 Tim. 6:17 God is a rich giver. | | Rom. 8:32 God is a free giver. | | John 3:16 God so loved us that He gave. |

It is God's will for all to be healed.

| Brazen serpent Passover lamb | | The words of Jesus | | The actions of Jesus | | The plan of redemption scriptures |

Figure 7.5

We have learned that the position to be in to obtain healing is the position of believing that we received when we prayed (Mark 11:24). However, in order to obtain this belief, knowledge is needed — knowledge that makes this belief possible to reach.

We began by learning that it is God's will for us to be well. We also learned that our willing God is a liberal giver. And finally, we learned that one method through which He gives is through the laying on of hands.

Each of these truths is vital if we are to comply with the requirements of Mark 11:24 — to believe that we receive when we pray.

A Summary

The belief that one method through which God gives healing is the laying on of hands is firmly established by Mark 6:1-6, Mark 8:22-25, Luke 4:40, and Mark 16:17-18. Together these scriptures give this belief the right to exist in our life.

Secondly, the truths that support this belief are to be given to others who find it difficult to believe that our God gives through the laying of hands. It becomes easy to persuade others about what we believe when what we believe has been established within us from the Word of God.

Thirdly, I remind you that the truths that support your belief must also be used to defend your belief. Once you believe that your Heavenly Father gives through the laying on of hands, there will be doubts that arise to question whether or not the laying on of hands was beneficial.

It becomes easy to persuade others about what we believe when what we believe has been established within us from the Word of God.

When these doubts arise, you must defend your beliefs by vocalizing what you know about your Heavenly Father. Quote the scripture passages that make up your beliefs. Defend your belief by saying, "But God gave to the people in his own hometown through the laying on of hands [Mark 6:1-6]. And He has given to me through the laying on of hands. God gave to the blind man through the laying on of hands [Mark 8:22-25]. And He has given to me through the laying on of hands." Doing this will cause the doubts to retreat, making it easier to remain loyal to your beliefs.

Dear reader, always remember that once a belief has been formed within you from God's Word, it is worth defending!

8
chapter

What God
Gives to the
Sick

Our failure to understand what God gives to the sick when hands are laid upon them has cost many their healing. Our lack of understanding as to what God gives is the main reason few ever step into the position of believing they receive when they pray.

Failure to understand this issue has caused many who have been prayed for to become disillusioned and frustrated. Some have been so disappointed that they no longer go forward to be prayed for because, according to them, "Nothing will happen, so what's the use."

This disappointment and frustration is the result of a lack of Bible knowledge.

We have allowed our experiences to develop unhealthy conclusions as to what God gives when hands are laid upon us without taking into consideration what the Word of God says about this subject.

Please read carefully what I am about to say.

What is the item sought after when people enter a healing line? What do the sick expect to receive when they pray? Is it not true that what the sick generally expect to receive is their healing manifestation? Decidedly, yes!

If what God gives is healing manifestations, then my question is this: Why would Jesus instruct us in Mark 11:24 to *believe that we receive* when we pray? It is obvious that if what God gives is a manifestation, then we would *know* that we have it. Therefore, believing that we received would be completely unnecessary.

The very fact that Jesus tells us to *believe* that we receive informs us clearly that when we pray we will not receive an instant manifestation.

That last statement is so important that I want to restate it using different words. When we obey Mark 11:24, Jesus did not promise us an instant manifestation. We know this because He said that when we pray we are to believe that we receive. *This indicates that there is going to be a period of time between the time we pray and the time it manifests that we are going to have to walk by what we believe and not by what we see.*

> *The very fact that Jesus tells us to believe that we receive informs us clearly that when we pray we will not receive an instant manifestation.*

So if healing manifestations are not what God gives, then what does God give to the sick when they pray or have hands laid upon them?

What God gives is the exact same ingredient that Jesus gave to the sick when He ministered upon the earth.

Jesus did not give one thing to the sick and the Father give something different. For if Jesus gave the sick one thing and the Father gives the sick something different, then we could examine what each gives, determine who gives the best gift, and then choose who to approach.

No, what Jesus gave to the sick is exactly what God gives to the sick today.

Jesus was God manifested in the flesh. Jesus said things like, "If you have seen Me, you've seen My Father. The words that I speak are not Mine but the Father's who sent me" (John 14:10).

Jesus said, *"I am come in my Father's name . . . "* (John 5:43). Through this statement, He was revealing to us that He was operating in a principle called the "power of attorney." The "power of attorney" is when one person comes on the behalf of another, in the name of another. It's just as if the person who sent him was there himself.

Jesus came as an ambassador of the Father. He represented the Father and carried out the Father's business upon the earth. What Jesus did while he was on the earth is exactly what the Father would do if He had come personally.

Do you understand that? Do you comprehend the fact that if the Father had come instead of Jesus he also would have said to Peter and John, "If you follow Me, I will make you fishers of men"? If the Father had come, He also would have taught His disciples. He also would have made clay from the spittle and told the man to go wash in the pool of Siloam. He also

Jesus came as an ambassador of the Father. He represented the Father and carried out the Father's business upon the earth.

would have marveled at the people's unbelief in His own hometown.

Jesus came in His Father's name. This is the reason Jesus said in John 13:20, *"Verily, verily, I say unto you, He that receiveth whomsoever I send receiveth me; and he that receiveth me receiveth him that sent me."* Jesus was acting, speaking, and healing on His Father's behalf. He did exactly what the Father would have done had He come to the earth Himself.

Jesus said in John 5:19, *". . . Verily, verily, I say unto you, The Son can do nothing of himself, but what he seeth the Father do: for what things soever he doeth, these also doeth the Son likewise."*

What did Jesus give the sick? Understand that Jesus could only give the sick what He has. If He doesn't have it, He can't give it.

For example, I personally could not give you a twenty-foot boat. Why? Because I don't have one. I couldn't give you a forty-acre ranch. Why? Because I don't have a forty-acre ranch. A person can only give what he has.

The same is true with Jesus. He could only give what He has. Consider this: If a sick person came to Jesus when Jesus was eleven years old, could Jesus have given him anything? (Be careful how you answer this!) Could Jesus have given the sick anything when He was eleven years of age?

The religious mind will immediately answer, "Yes!" But wait a minute, Philippians 2:7 and 8 provide us with some vital information concerning Jesus. This passage informs us that when Jesus came into this world, He stripped Himself of all His heavenly privileges and rightful dignity and became as a man. Philippians 2:7 and 8 says, *"But made himself of no reputation, and took upon him the form of a servant, and was made in the likeness of men: And being found in fashion as a man, he humbled himself, and became obedient unto death, even the death of the cross."*

Jesus did not operate on this earth as God, but rather He operated on this earth as a man. Let's read what Luke 2:52 says about Jesus' early developmental years: *"And Jesus increased in wisdom and stature, and in favour with God and man."* If Jesus possessed everything He had before He came into the world, He would not have needed to increase in wisdom and stature, and in favour with God.

The Bible plainly teaches that when Jesus came into the earth, He came as a man. With that in mind, let's return to the question: Could Jesus have given the sick anything at the age of eleven? The answer is a shocking, "No!" Could He have given anything to the sick at the age of twenty-two? Once again, the answer is, "No!" Could He have given anything to the sick at the age of twenty-nine? No!

From the birth of Jesus until He was baptized in the Jordan River by John, Jesus did no miracles. Why? He didn't have anything to give those who were in need of a miracle.

But then, at the age of thirty, the Bible tells us in Acts 10:38, *"How God anointed Jesus of Nazareth with the Holy Ghost and with power: who went about doing good, and healing all that were oppressed of the devil; for God was with him."*

Jesus was anointed with the Holy Ghost and power when He was baptized by John in the Jordan River. It was during this baptismal service that God gave to Jesus things that He had never possessed before. Peter enlightens us in Acts 10:38 as to what Jesus was given during this baptism. He was given the Holy Ghost and power.

From that point on, Jesus had something to give the sick when they came to Him. He either gave them manifestations of the Holy Ghost, as the Holy Ghost willed (1 Cor. 12:11), or He gave them some of this power.

What kind of power was this that Jesus was anointed with? It must have been healing power due to the fact that He went about doing good and healing all that were oppressed of the devil (Acts 10:38).

As a result of this anointing, Jesus had one of two things that he could give the sick when they came to him. He could give them manifestations of the Holy Ghost, as the Spirit wills, or He could give them some of this healing power.

God Gives Healing Power

What does God give the sick today when hands are laid on them? He gives them healing power. The instant we pray or hands are laid upon us, the healing power of God is administered to our body.

Therefore, after we pray we can confidently proclaim that we believe that we received. Our bold confession is not based on what we see or feel. Rather, our confession is based on the solid foundation that it is God's will for us to be well, that He is a liberal giver, that He gives through the laying on of hands, and that what He gives is healing power.

Let's add this principle to our visual illustration. It is so easy to believe that we receive when we have the proper foundation underneath us (Fig. 8.1).

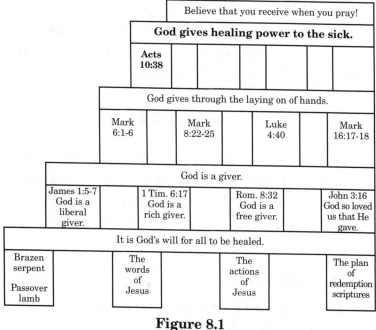

	Believe that you receive when you pray!				
	God gives healing power to the sick.				
Acts 10:38					

God gives through the laying on of hands.				
Mark 6:1-6	Mark 8:22-25	Luke 4:40	Mark 16:17-18

God is a giver.			
James 1:5-7 God is a liberal giver.	1 Tim. 6:17 God is a rich giver.	Rom. 8:32 God is a free giver.	John 3:16 God so loved us that He gave.

It is God's will for all to be healed.			
Brazen serpent / Passover lamb	The words of Jesus	The actions of Jesus	The plan of redemption scriptures

Figure 8.1

We are talking about the God-side of healing. It is clear from our visual illustration (Fig. 8.1) that what the sick need to know about our God is the following: (1) Our God is willing to heal all; (2) Our God is a giver; (3) One method through which He gives is through the laying on of hands; and (4) What He gives is healing power.

Do you understand why so many are having difficulty believing they receive when they pray? It is because of a lack of knowledge as to these foundational truths. Once this foundation is laid within us, entering into the realm of believing that we receive when we pray is well within our reach.

Healing Power

I want to provide the scriptural support that will form the belief within us that what God gives to the sick is healing power. We have already provided the first support, which is Acts 10:38. The second support passage concerning this truth is found in the Gospel of Mark.

Mark 5:25-34

In the Gospel of Mark we are given the story of the woman with the issue of blood. As we read this account, we must ask ourselves two questions: What did she come to receive? And what did she receive when she touched Jesus?

MARK 5:25-34

25 And a certain woman, which had an issue of blood twelve years,

26 And had suffered many things of many physicians, and had spent all that she had, and was nothing bettered, but rather grew worse,

27 When she had heard of Jesus, came in the press behind, and touched his garment.

28 For she said, If I may touch but his clothes, I shall be whole.

29 And straightway the fountain of her blood was dried up; and she felt in her body that she was healed of that plague.

30 And Jesus, immediately knowing in himself that virtue had gone out of him, turned him about in the press, and said, Who touched my clothes?

31 And his disciples said unto him, Thou seest the multitude thronging thee, and sayest thou, Who touched me?

32 And he looked round about to see her that had done this thing.

33 But the woman fearing and trembling, knowing what was done in her, came and fell down before him, and told him all the truth.

34 And he said unto her, Daughter, thy faith hath made thee whole; go in peace, and be whole of thy plague.

What she came to obtain is found in verse 28: *"For she said, If I may touch but his clothes, I shall be whole."* She came to be made whole. She came to be healed.

What did she receive when she touched the hem of His garment? Verse 30 provides the answer. It says, *"And Jesus, immediately knowing in himself that virtue had gone out of him, turned him about in the press, and said, Who touched my clothes?"* She came to be made whole, but when she touched Jesus

Once this foundation is laid within us, entering into the realm of believing that we receive when we pray is well within our reach.

she was given "virtue." The instant she touched Him, virtue flowed out of Him into her.

What is this virtue? The word "virtue" means *power*. What kind of power went out of Him? It must have been healing power because it healed her.

Notice that it did not say that when she touched Him, a healing manifestation flowed from Him to her. It said plainly that what flowed out of Him when she touched Him was *healing power*.

The healing power had to be administered first. This made her manifestation possible. Dear reader, do you understand? Before manifestations are possible, the healing power of God must be administered and believed by the recipient that it was received.

She came to receive her healing, but what flowed from Him was healing power. This healing power is the same power that is spoken of in Acts 10:38. Jesus was anointed with it when He was baptized by John in the Jordan River.

Before manifestations are possible, the healing power of God must be administered and believed by the recipient that it was received.

If *she* received virtue, or in other words, healing power, from Jesus, then healing power will be what *we* receive from our Heavenly Father when we approach Him for healing. Jesus is not going to give one thing to the woman with the issue of blood and then the Father give something totally different to you and I when we are in need of healing.

Let's add this support scripture to our visual illustration (Fig. 8.2).

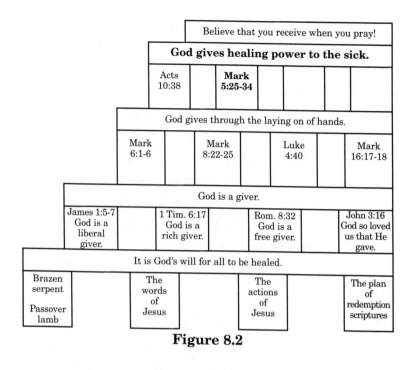

Figure 8.2

Luke 6:17-19

Lets look at another story that will help us further understand that what God gives is healing power. Luke 6:17-19 says, *"And he came down with them, and stood in the plain, and the company of his disciples, and a great multitude of people out of all Judaea and Jerusalem, and from the sea coast of Tyre and Sidon, which came to hear him, and to be healed of their diseases; And they that were vexed with unclean spirits: and they were healed. And the whole multitude sought to touch him: for there went virtue out of him, and healed them all."*

Once again, we find the sick coming to Jesus to be healed. What they were given is revealed in the following: *"And the whole multitude sought to touch him: for there* went *virtue out of him, and healed them all*" (Luke 6:19). Again, the word "virtue" means *power*. What kind of power was this? It must have been healing power due to the fact that the sick were healed.

What they were given was *healing power*. It did not say that they were given *healing manifestations*. And yet, isn't that what most are believing that they are going to receive when they are prayed for in healing lines today? However, healing power is what the sick received when they came to Jesus. And healing power is what the sick will receive today when they obey Mark 11:24.

Let's add this scriptural passage to our visual illustration (Fig. 8.3).

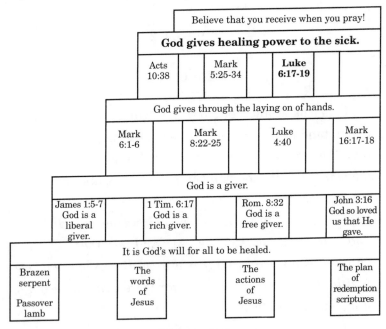

Figure 8.3

Luke 5:17

The fourth and final support passage that enables us to form the belief within us that God gives healing power is found in Luke 5:17: *"And it came to pass on a certain day, as he was teaching, that there were Pharisees and doctors of the law sitting by, which were come out of every town of Galilee, and Judaea, and Jerusalem: and the power of the Lord was present to heal them."*

Notice that it did not say that their healing manifestations were present. It plainly said that the power of the Lord was present to heal them. Therefore, we can conclude that what God gives the sick is healing power. So let's add this support passage to our visual illustration (Fig. 8.4).

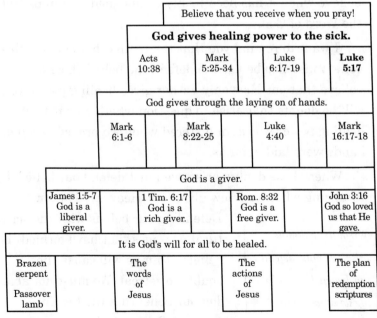

Figure 8.4

Now that we understand *what* God gives, our reaction after we pray should be quite different than before this understanding was obtained. Before we understood what God gives, the moment we said "amen," we began to examine our bodies to determine whether or not God gave our manifestation to us.

However, now that we have received this truth, the instant we hear the word "amen," we can lift our hands and begin to express thanks for the power that was administered to our bodies. We are now acting as the result of what we believe and not by what we see. Glory!

These scriptural passages can be given to others who find it difficult to believe that what our God gives is healing power. It becomes easy to persuade others about what we believe when it has been firmly established within us from the Word of God.

I want to remind you that the truths that support this belief must also be used to defend the belief. Once we believe that our Heavenly Father gives healing power, there will be doubts that arise to question whether or not the healing power was administered when we prayed or when hands were laid upon us.

When these doubts arise, we must defend our beliefs by vocalizing what we know about our Heavenly Father.

When these doubts arise, we must defend our beliefs by vocalizing what we know about our Heavenly Father.

Defending our beliefs with the scriptural passages that have formed the belief within us will cause the doubts to retreat. We must not abandon our belief that the healing power of God was administered to our bodies the instant hands were laid upon us.

chapter

'Believing That You Receive' Made Easy

Looking one more time to our visual illustration (Fig. 9.1), it now becomes easy to comply with the instructions given in Mark 11:24: *". . . What things soever ye desire, when ye pray, believe that ye receive them, and ye shall have them."*

Knowing that our God is willing, that He gives through the laying on of hands, and that what He gives is healing power enables us to step into the realm of believing that we receive when we pray. Also, these truths provide us with enough knowledge about our Father that we are able to continue believing that we received until we are satisfied with the fruit produced.

Remaining in the belief that we received when we prayed demands that every thought and suggestion about the outcome be scrutinized, or examined. Any thought that questions whether or not we received must be responded to immediately. Failure to do so could result in the entertainment of thoughts that would eventually cause us to drift away from believing that we received or denounce the belief all together.

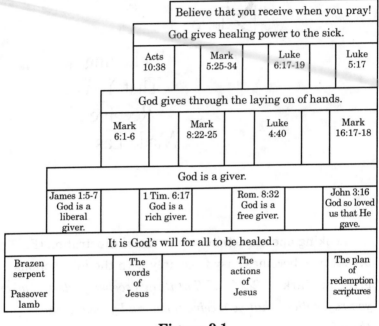

Believe that you receive when you pray!			
God gives healing power to the sick.			
Acts 10:38	Mark 5:25-34	Luke 6:17-19	Luke 5:17
God gives through the laying on of hands.			
Mark 6:1-6	Mark 8:22-25	Luke 4:40	Mark 16:17-18
God is a giver.			
James 1:5-7 God is a liberal giver.	1 Tim. 6:17 God is a rich giver.	Rom. 8:32 God is a free giver.	John 3:16 God so loved us that He gave.
It is God's will for all to be healed.			
Brazen serpent Passover lamb	The words of Jesus	The actions of Jesus	The plan of redemption scriptures

Figure 9.1

The thought will come, "You really didn't get anything when you prayed, did you?" (Notice that this thought is not questioning whether or not it is God's will to heal you. Rather, this thought is questioning whether or not God gave to you when you prayed. Its purpose is to cause you to question whether or not you received and ultimately cause you to stop believing that you received when you prayed.)

When thoughts such as this occur, immediately begin to vocalize what your beliefs are founded upon. Your response to such a thought should be sharp and immediate. Your response to such a thought should be full of the scriptures

Remaining in the belief that we received when we prayed demands that every thought and suggestion about the outcome be scrutinized, or examined.

that make up your beliefs. The scriptures that have formed your beliefs must now be turned into a sword to defend your position.

A proper response to such a question would sound something like this: "Now wait a minute. My Father is a giver and a liberal one at that [James 1:5]. He gives freely [Rom. 8:32] and He gives richly [1 Tim. 6:17]. Not only that, but He gave me the healing power of God when hands were laid on me. The same healing power that was administered to the woman with the issue of blood [Mark 5:30] was administered to my body when hands were laid on me. The same virtue or healing power that flowed out of Jesus in Luke 6:19 is in me working mightily. I believe that I received when I prayed. Glory!"

Do you understand, my dear friend? We must vocalize what we believe in much the same way Jesus dealt with the thoughts that Satan hurled at him during the three temptations found in the Gospel of Luke.

LUKE 4:1-13

1 And Jesus being full of the Holy Ghost returned from Jordan, and was led by the Spirit into the wilderness,

2 Being forty days tempted of the devil. And in those days he did eat nothing: and when they were ended, he afterward hungered.

3 And the devil said unto him, If thou be the Son of God, command this stone that it be made bread.

4 And Jesus answered him, saying, IT IS WRITTEN, That man shall not live by bread alone, but by every word of God.

5 And the devil, taking him up into an high mountain, shewed unto him all the kingdoms of the world in a moment of time.

6 And the devil said unto him, All this power will I give thee, and the glory of them: for that is delivered unto me; and to whomsoever I will I give it.

7 If thou therefore wilt worship me, all shall be thine.

8 And Jesus answered and said unto him, Get thee behind me, Satan: for IT IS WRITTEN, Thou shalt worship the Lord thy God, and him only shalt thou serve.

9 And he brought him to Jerusalem, and set him on a pinnacle of the temple, and said unto him, If thou be the Son of God, cast thyself down from hence:

10 For it is written, He shall give his angels charge over thee, to keep thee:

11 And in their hands they shall bear thee up, lest at any time thou dash thy foot against a stone.

12 And Jesus answering said unto him, IT IS SAID, Thou shalt not tempt the Lord thy God.

13 And when the devil had ended all the temptation, he departed from him for a season.

In verse 4, Jesus responds to the thought with the words, "It is written." Again, in verse 8, He responds boldly, "It is written." Lastly, in verse 12, He says, "It is said."

We must vocalize what we believe. We must confess what we believe. We must follow the example of our Lord and speak what we believe when confronted with thoughts that question whether or not we received when we prayed.

Thanksgiving: The Only Thing Left To Do

One way to continually keep what we believe in front of us is to express to our Father how grateful we are for the following four things:

1) For making us aware of the fact that it is His will to heal all.

2) For informing us that He is a liberal, rich, and free giver.

3) For showing us that one way He gives is through the laying on of hands.

4) For revealing to us that what He gives is the healing power of God.

Every time you think of it, give thanks concerning these issues. Doing so will increase your ability to remain loyal to the beliefs that have been formed within you from God's

Word. Thanksgiving will also keep your beliefs in the forefront of your mind.

Once that power is administrated, the only thing left to do is give thanks. For thanksgiving is the polite thing to do once we realize that something has been given to us.

Think about that last paragraph for a moment. We often see people leaving prayer lines not thanking God, but rather looking to see if anything has changed. They are looking to see if they were given their manifestation. But those who know their God — how He gives and what He gives — will look up toward Heaven and offer thanks the instant hands are laid upon them. They know that the healing power of God was administered to them and is working in them mightily. They are walking by what they believe and not by what they see.

> *Thanksgiving will . . . keep your beliefs in the forefront of your mind.*

From the instant we pray until we are satisfied with our physical condition, our faith and confession must be the result of what we believe. We must daily remind ourselves of the scriptures that make up our beliefs. We must daily remind ourselves that the healing power of God was administered to our body when we prayed. Then we can continually give thanks because we *believe that we received when we prayed.*

10

A Final
Word of
Encouragement

The position of believing that we receive is a position that takes effort to enter into. A time of learning is required in order to enter into this position. And once the position is achieved, it must be maintained. Therefore, I encourage you to continually feed on the scriptures that make up the foundation of each belief. Maintain your beliefs by continually offering thanks to God concerning each belief. And above all, when thoughts arise that go against what you believe, vocalize the scriptures that make up the foundation of each belief. Doing so will cause you to remain in proper position.

Maintain Your Relationship With Your Medical Physician

As you continue to stand your ground, I encourage you to also remain under the care of your medical physicians. Do what they encourage you to do. Continue to take the medication as prescribed by your physicians. And every time you take that pill or drink that medication, say, "I believe that the healing power was administered. I believe that it is at work within me mightily. I believe that I received when I prayed."

Yield to the Leadership of the Holy Spirit

Also, as you find yourself walking in the realm of believing that you received when you prayed, I encourage you to remain sensitive to the Holy Spirit. He is the One who will lead you into all truth. If there is an area in your life that needs to be adjusted, I am confident that the Holy Spirit will reveal it to you. When an area is exposed, make the adjustment quickly. If you need to ask for God's forgiveness according to First John 1:9, then ask for it. If you need to reconcile with a spouse, friend, or acquaintance, I believe the Lord will reveal it to you and will show you what to do.

If there is an area in your life that needs to be adjusted, I am confident that the Holy Spirit will reveal it to you.

Over the years I have observed many who think that the only thing they need to do in order to be healed is to forgive all those they have offended or who have offended them. However, you can live a clean life — free from strife — and still remain bound to sickness if you have not believed you have received when you prayed.

On the other hand, I have witnessed those who have believed they received when they prayed, but while they were in this position, the Holy Spirit was dealing with them about a strained relationship in which they needed to forgive a person.

Dear reader, if the Holy Spirit reveals an area in your life that you need to adjust, I encourage you to yield to Him. I discovered a long time ago that apologizing to another person is a small price to pay in order to enjoy health. Forsaking sin is a small price to pay in order to be strong physically.

Lastly

Finally, examine yourself. Take time to locate yourself. Ask yourself the following questions: Where am I in relationship to the realm of believing that I received when I prayed? Am I in this realm with its proper foundation or am I still trying to *get* God to heal me? Am I maintaining my position of believing that I received properly or have I allowed thoughts to lead me away from this belief?

> *Forsaking sin is a small price to pay in order to be strong physically.*

My prayer for you, my friend, is that you will move yourself into the position of believing that you received and that you will be in health even as your soul has prospered through what you have learned in this book. May the grace of our Heavenly Father be with you and all that you set your hand to do.

THE Word of Faith

The Word of Faith is a full-color magazine
with faith-building teaching articles by
Rev. Kenneth E. Hagin and Rev. Kenneth Hagin Jr.

The Word of Faith also includes encouraging true-life
stories of Christians overcoming circumstances
through God's Word, and information on the
various outreaches of Kenneth Hagin Ministries
and RHEMA Bible Church.

To receive a free subscription to *The Word of Faith*, call:

1-888-28-FAITH
(1-888-283-2484)
www.rhema.org

RHEMA
Bible Training Center

Want to reach the height of your potential?

RHEMA can take you there.

| *proven instructors*
| *alumni benefits*
| *career placement*
| *hands-on experience*
| *curriculum you can use*

Do you desire —

- to find and effectively fulfill God's plan for your life?
- to know how to "rightly divide the Word of truth"?
- to learn how to follow and flow with the Spirit of God?
- to run your God-given race with excellence and integrity?
- to become not only a laborer but a *skilled* laborer?

If so, then RHEMA Bible Training Center is here for you!

For a free video and full-color catalog, call:

1-888-28-FAITH
(1-888-283-2484)

www.rhema.org

RHEMA Bible Training Center admits students of any race, color, or ethnic origin.

RHEMA
Correspondence Bible School

• Flexible •

Enroll anytime: choose your topic of study; study at your own pace!

• Affordable •

Pay as you go — only $25 per lesson!

(Price subject to change without notice.)

• Profitable •

"Words cannot adequately describe the tremendous impact RCBS has had on my life. I have learned so much, and I am always sharing my newfound knowledge with everyone I can. I feel like a blind person who has just had his eyes opened!"

Louisiana

"RCBS has been a stepping-stone in my growing faith to serve God with the authority that He has given the Church over all the power of the enemy!"

New York

The RHEMA Correspondence Bible School is a home Bible study course that can help you in your everyday life!

This course of study has been designed with the layman in mind, with practical teaching on prayer, faith, healing, Spirit-led living, and much more to help you live a victorious Christian life!

For enrollment information and course listing call today!

1-888-28-FAITH
(1-888-283-2484)

www.rhema.org